G000253430

It is high time for this book. D'
poor teaching and bad exam
either afraid of prophets or want nothing to do with them
at all. The church is thus missing the glorious voice of the
Bridegroom to his bride. Keith Hazell is one of the very few
who is uniquely equipped to share this accurate vision of the
role and purpose of the New Testament prophet. I pray that,
somehow, every person called to the prophetic and every
church leader would eventually imbibe what is in this very
important book. Understanding the things written here are
a key to the health and future of the Christian Church.

Pete Beck, Jr, *Apostolic leadership team, Master Builders
Fellowship of Churches North Carolina, USA*

Keith Hazell delivers a very practical and personal treatise
that will help build correct internal platforms for the
accurate and orderly delivery of Christ's prophetic grace.
Traveling with Keith for many years, I received tutelage
and consistent demonstration of the ethics, values,
protocol and theology that prophetic ministry must
operate from. Reading this book will craft your life, not
just your gift.

Dr Clem Ferris, *Prophet, Apostolic team of Grace
Churches International, North Carolina, USA*

This is a challenging and inspirational masterpiece on
the nature, roles and importance of mature prophetic
ministry for effective 21st century New Testament church
life. Drawing from rich wells of experience, wisdom and
revelation, Keith's work is a must-read for the prophetically
inclined, seasoned prophets, and church leaders at all levels.

Ben Goodman, *Prophetic minister, Life Links International
Churches, Grace Churches International and Truebridge
Churches, Minnesota USA*

Keith Hazell is a recognized prophet who is well-positioned to write this book on prophetic ministry. Keith has done a lot over the years to explain, demonstrate and restore the proper function of the New Testament prophet to the body of Christ. This book embodies the practical teaching of the prophetic that Keith has so lived out over 40 years of ministry. It will bless and enrich you as you read and study this excellent book! I highly recommend it!

Dave Wells, *Team leader, Life Links International Churches, Regina SK Canada*

I love it when fathers speak and Keith is one of the prophetic fathers I listen to. With a long track record of accuracy and integrity I am encouraged that we finally have some of his wisdom, encouragement and caution penned in this book. It will leave a legacy for the next generation of New Testament prophets. This book is jam packed with fresh revelation, careful instruction and robust faith. It will help anybody discover what authentic prophetic ministry, working alongside the apostolic should look like in the mission minded local church. Buy it, it will do you good!

Julian Adams, *Prophet, working with Newfrontiers, UK and internationally*

Written by one of the most fruitful prophetic mentors in our generation, this book is filled with a deep love for the body of Christ and a passion to see the prophetic accurately modelled and taught. With decades of experience and insight, this book will help you to understand prophetic ministry as it was meant to be.

Richard Kao, *Senior pastor, Fivestones Church, Vancouver Canada*

Whose word is it anyway?

Receiving and acting on personal and corporate prophecy

About the author

Keith Hazell and his wife Nova live in Lethbridge, Alberta, Canada and are based in Mosaic Church. Keith has been in prophetic ministry for more than 40 years and ministers extensively at home and abroad. He and his wife are British born and have strong roots in eastern England.

Lastword Publications
Lowestoft, Suffolk, UK
www.lastwordpublications.com

First published 2011, by Lastword Publications
www.lastwordpublications.com
Lastword Publications works with authors and musicians, businesses and charities to provide professional results with maximum impact.

ISBN 978 0 9559439 6 6

Useful website links:
www.relationalmission.com
www.newfrontierstogether.org

Design and production by The Upper Room (London, UK) 020 8406 1010

Contents

Foreword

Just how does a local church know what to do? What programs to run, whom to release into ministry, what buildings to buy and where to put their missional efforts? Do the leadership team gather their brightest and best in a room with a flipchart and marker pen to come up with the best creative ideas their minds can muster? And how does an individual seeking to please God with their life make choices of where to go, what to do and who to work with?

Certainly the wisdom of God and the scriptures are key ways God guides us as church and individuals, but the New Testament reveals a third component flavouring the emerging church. We see Paul attempting to go to a planned destination, only to have a divine encounter where God speaks prophetically through a vision about a whole new direction for his ministry. Elsewhere, Paul encourages Timothy to work hard at developing his gifting and reminds him that his calling to serve God in leadership was ignited through prophetic words.

As valuable as the prophetic gift is, it is also dangerous. History is littered with abuses and excesses. How we need authentic ministry manifested in God-honouring lives. Used correctly, the gift will always edify, encourage, strengthen and console. It will have a building effect on the lives of those who are touched by it, even when correction or adjustment is required.

I have known Keith Hazell for over 20 years and in that time have come to love him as a friend and honour him as a genuine prophet. He hears from God regularly and consistently and I have observed up close how he lives his life: his passion for people, availability to God and devotion to the scriptures of doctrine. He loves the church and desires for her to become all God wants her to be. This is no remote and melancholic figure somewhat withdrawn from life – Keith is the life and soul of the party!

I have encouraged Keith for many years to write a book that will in some way enshrine the values he has lived by and also entrust into the hands of others some wonderful foundations for the coming years. I trust and pray that many more like Keith will be raised up to bring the much needed clear voice and direction of God into the lives of churches and individual followers of Christ.

Mike Betts *Lowestoft, England 2011*

Introduction

'Faith is the substance of things hoped for, the evidence of things not seen.'

I have attempted to write this book many times during the years of my involvement in prophetic ministry. Many have urged me to write down my thoughts and insights and share them with those who follow after me. Past attempts have landed in failure and frustration but now finally the 'substance' has arrived!

More than 40 years in prophetic ministry have allowed me to see a massive climate change in the body of Christ towards present day prophetic revelation being readily accepted. However, I have also witnessed many deviations from basic scriptural teaching and much bizarre outworking of what is considered to be prophetic. My desire is to bring clarity concerning the role of New Testament prophets and prophetic ministry. Used correctly these gifts are invaluable to both churches and individuals whereas their abuse or neglect often cause great harm.

In the process of a life of international ministry my feet have touched the ground in many continents and I owe a debt to all who have received and supported me in prayer and finances. I have also been blessed with much help from prophetic men and I in turn have sought to teach others entering this ministry. To mention names would be superfluous since most would not recognise them as prominent, but they have been dynamically successful out of the eyes of the sensation seekers. By this I mean that we have been happy to help build church in obscurity rather than seeking to inflate our own personal ministry by simply seeking the spotlight and huge recognition. This is not to say we have only sought to minister in churches of a handful, but have also been blessed to prophesy in churches of thousands.

The reproduction of all kinds of prophetic ministry has been a passion with me and I rejoice to see younger men and women that I have mentored going beyond me in both revelation and insight. The joy of working in teams and not alone has so blessed me as I travelled and ministered in so many churches and lands. To see local churches welcoming and benefiting from New Testament prophets is a great delight indeed.

I was helped initially in editing my thoughts by an old friend Peter White of City Hill Church in Eden Prairie MN. Following these initial outlines, Phil Stoddart of Lastword made himself available to pilot the project through and put many hours of adjustment into my writing style and presentation. I cannot thank him enough, for without him I fear this publication would merely have been a manuscript perhaps discovered and published long after I was off the scene!

Phil has reason to encourage the writing of this book and for his participation since, at a time of great tragedy in his own life, God gave me a prophetic word that he and his wife would author a book. Out of that word came the recognition of a need to have a publisher and Lastword was born. Since their book *A12 To Heaven,* a number more have followed of which mine is the latest.

Keith Hazell *Lethbridge, Canada 2011*

Dedication

I dedicate this book to my wife Nova who for more than 50 years has walked alongside me loving and praying for me and bringing encouragement at every step. She has been friend, confidante and fellow labourer and has especially encouraged me to produce this book.

Also to my son Jeremy who has been my supporter and co-worker for many years; to my daughters, Anita and Nicola, who sometimes had trouble explaining to teachers and friends that their dad was a prophet. All three are gifted with prophetic insight in different ways. Along with Nova they have suffered my long absences on mission around the world without complaint and have never failed to support me in all my efforts whether successful or not. Truly I am a blessed man.

Keith *October 2011*

1 Supernaturally searching

Normally the speedway stadium in Rayleigh, Essex operated like any other in the UK, but not tonight. Rather than the usual roaring of motorbikes and the cheers of a few thousand spectators for the blue and yellow-clad riders called the Rayleigh Rockets, a crowd of similar size gathered to hear the man from America.

It was March 1954 and the reputation of Billy Graham's evangelistic meetings had attracted my attention. Operating under the umbrella title of 'The Greater London Crusade' a series of evening meetings and special events were planned for Hyde Park, Trafalgar Square, US army camps and various other places. By the end of the three month long crusade, some 120,000 packed into Wembley Stadium and around 60,000 into the nearby White City Stadium.

In the previous week I had taken advantage of a free bus ride to the Haringay arena, a greyhound racing track in London that seated around 12,000 people. That night I sat there as a young man, discovering for the first time that there was more to life than imagined. Up to this moment God only existed as vague concept, floating somewhere beyond the grasp of human experience. But now I was learning specifically about this elusive entity and that communication with him at a personal level was possible. Never before had the sacrifice of Jesus Christ seemed so significant: the realisation that God could come and live right inside of me was nothing short of mind-blowing. Words such as 'converted' and 'born again' took on a real, wonderful and powerful meaning. Something within me responded and cried out silently to God.

Hungry for more, I was now packed in with the crowd at Rayleigh, listening to an associate of Billy called Grady Wilson.

This time I was going to go to the front when the call came from the platform to make a stand for Christ. It wasn't enough just to make the commitment in my heart, I had to do it publicly – for my sake just as much as anyone looking on. I wanted to be visibly identified as someone who had changed.

From that night on, seeking after God and growing in this new-found faith became my primary focus and soon I was part of a group of zealous young men and women looking for the evidence of God's reality in a tangible way. One day, during lunch break at High School, one of my new friends told me that tonight he was invited to a meeting where God would speak. But living in a rural area annoyingly meant I couldn't attend as the last bus home left too early. So, a long impatient wait followed until the next day when at least I could hear second-hand what had happened.

My mind was almost bursting with anticipation when the story could finally be heard. He recounted going to a house and meeting with a dozen other people who all wanted to hear God speak. A water glass was placed upside down in the centre of a dining table and those present invited to join hands to ask the glass questions for 'God would answer'.

My friend being zealous took his Bible with him and when there was no response from the glass, he simply raised his Bible over the glass in an attempt to encourage God! As soon as this happened the glass exploded violently sending pieces all around the room! Perhaps unsurprisingly they asked him to leave immediately, which he did so, being very puzzled about the whole affair.

The quest for the supernatural continued unabated as we sought to discover an authentic manifestation of the real presence and voice of God. Only a few months later a group of us were walking in the high street of a nearby town when a man approached with a pamphlet in his hands inviting us to a healing meeting. The leaflet proclaimed 'all are welcome', so of course we felt able to go along with confidence. Several of us in the group had Bibles in our hands and on entering were directed to the back row of the meeting.

After a while, people rose from their wooden seats and proceeded to the front for healing and we as new believers prayed most fervently for them in the name of Jesus. Some 45 minutes later, the leader of the meeting announced in a rather irritated tone that, due to resistance on the part of some in the crowd, 'the spirits' were unable to bring about healings in the manner in which they were accustomed. The next thing we knew he had fingered us out as the culprits 'resisting' and told in no uncertain terms to leave immediately.

Why do I tell you these two stories? My purpose is to let you know two things:

- Everything supernatural is not from God
- There is evidently that which is supernatural that resists the Bible and the name of Jesus and which is suppressed by either of them.
- There is evidently that which is supernatural that resists the Bible and the name of Jesus and which, in fact, is directly contradicted by them both.

A magnificent obsession?

Many young people – and for that matter older ones – are obsessed with the supernatural today and are searching for some manifestation of supernatural reality in our present age. Ouija boards and satanic role-playing games seem a plausible and direct gateway to the supernatural world. Yet all that they find is a world of paths without signposts and all leading to despair and disillusionment.

However, the presence of the false always implies there is a genuine and the Bible both confirms and teaches us to be aware of the false which always attempts to mislead and corrupt. No one is immune from this, particularly those searching for reality, who in ignorance and innocence, are drawn into the wrong supernatural realm.

The Bible[1] gives guidance with these words from 1 John 4: 1: *Dear friends, do not believe every spirit, but test the spirits to see whether they are from God, because many false prophets have gone out into the world.*

John is in no doubt that the realm of supernatural revelation and reality can proceed from two sources. He urges the reader to be aware of this and to make the appropriate checks before becoming involved and maybe trapped.

When working in London for a Lloyds insurance broker I used to take my own lunch and eat with the rest of the staff every day. One day as we were eating, a young woman at the table complained of a bad backache. As we continued to talk about this, the Holy Spirit began to speak to me about her, saying that she was a spiritual medium and the pain in her back was where a spirit of divination entered her body.

I would have been happy to keep the information to myself but the Holy Spirit urged me to tell her about why she had the pain. Immediately, she became defensive and asked, "Who told you that?" My response was to ask if it were the case. She replied that the only other person who had said that to her was another spiritual medium with the very same problem.

The story that followed told of how one day her grandmother had inducted her into the world of the spirits when her own mother was out shopping. She had not told anyone until later on when her brother died. Upon hearing about it, the rest of the family begged her to contact that brother who had died so tragically young. For her part she was reluctant but nevertheless began the process of trying to call up the dead spirit because the spirit of divination that had possessed her grandmother was also available to her.

[1] All Bible references are from the New International Version, unless otherwise noted

From that point on she became enslaved and experienced continual physical pain in her back for which there was no relief. I told her of the One who could deliver her and offered proof of greater supernatural power. By revelation, I told her that she would go home and before bed she would come within inches of losing her life but would not be touched.

Next day at the table she told me of going after supper to buy some treats for her children from an ice cream truck. As she stepped out from behind the van a speeding car came along and knocked both ice creams from her hand but did not touch her physically. To my surprise, even after this clear demonstration of the overwhelming power of God, she was unwilling to surrender her life to Christ.

Perhaps she doubted that she would really be freed from the pain or was unwilling to give up the control and power she felt from that spirit. Whatever her reasons, she chose to continue being a pawn of the spirit which blinded her eyes and ears to the Gospel.

Supernatural Church

I have even encountered Christians with horror stories about their attempts to become involved with the supernatural. It is not just those without faith who have been ensnared by their own naivety or curiosity. Sadly, those seeking supernatural experience search in many places but rarely expect to find fulfilment in their local church. Sometimes this has been due to lack of encouragement.

Regrettably, my own quest for the supernatural was soon diverted when I became a part of an evangelical church that taught about historical supernatural experiences, but insisted such things had clearly now ceased. Unsurprisingly, the church lacked any current experience of the moving of the Holy Spirit. Sadly many denominational churches are still closed to the gifts and actions of the Holy Spirit today.

They are a testimony to what happens when people become involved with teaching the Word but simultaneously reject the ongoing moving of the Holy Spirit in power.

In my own life, as the years continued, there was a hunger in my spirit to see what I termed 'the evident power that the apostles enjoyed in the New Testament'. I was clear in my prayers to God that this was what I wanted but without any 'speaking in tongues' as this was undoubtedly satanic – or so I had been most convincingly assured.

However, a little short of my thirtieth birthday I had an unexpected 'encounter of a supernatural kind'. It was one that went on to revolutionize my life and set me upon a path that would seek to encourage the supernatural manifestations of the Holy Spirit inside the protective covering of the church. A friend of mine puts it this way: "The fire and manifestation of the Holy Spirit is best contained within the fireplace of the local church where God intended it to be."

But, let me set the stage a little around the 'encounter'. I was (and still am) passionately concerned with the nations and the spreading of the Gospel. At that time, this passion led my wife and I to become representatives of a zealous faith missionary society working in the heart of Africa.

One Easter I attended a house party with around 20 others as part of a 'holiness mission'. Early on Easter Sunday morning we rose for a sunrise service and to partake in communion. But our anticipation of having a time of repentance and prayer did not happen as planned.

While we were praying, the Holy Spirit came into the room and every person was sovereignly and immediately filled with divine power and presence. Additionally, everyone spoke with tongues; well everyone except me! God, who does answer prayer, remembered mine. I received as requested the anointing of the Apostles, but no 'speaking in tongues'.

At the very next meeting I was preaching in a Baptist church and discerned that five people would be saved. In my altar call, I indicated their gender and where they were sitting in the hall. To my surprise, they all stood in the places as I had noted! I came to realise in the next few months that this was the first evidence of being given a strong prophetic gift from God. This gift would bring me much joy … and much trouble!!

Things began to happen as those months passed and finally when I heard another person prophesy in a Pentecostal church meeting, I realized that this was my gift too. After a few more months I began to speak in tongues and could probably have done so at the initial experience if it were not for being so hung up with the false teaching I had received.

Back on home soil, this experience was hard to import into the evangelical church that I had joined. I found myself excluded from preaching there at all, having been 'tarred with the brush of heresy'. But none of the hostility experienced put out the fire in my heart to see this anointing expressed in the context of the local church. If there was not a church to receive such things, I would work with others to build one where these things would be a welcome part of church life as they should be.

In these words from 1 Corinthians 12: 28a, Paul clearly points to the authentic supernatural revelation and power being provided by God through the avenue of the church:
And in the church God has appointed first of all apostles, second prophets, third teachers, then workers of miracles, also those having gifts of healing.

There is no indication of such provisions ceasing or expiring with the deaths of the first apostles. And so it came as quite a relief to discover that I was not the only one to desire such a church: one that looked like those in the New Testament. In fact, a careful study of history shows they have been in existence all throughout time since the churches of the

New Testament. [2] Such churches are called New Testament Churches because they use the New Testament as their guide both for the form of government of the church and for the basis of the sort of meetings they hold. They allow and expect the Holy Spirit to move in the same way as the Bible says he has always moved and in which he will continue to move.

Since then I have worked alongside others with the same vision and purpose to see a manifestation of such a church. It is the reason for writing this book about prophets and prophecy. My desire is to bring people, inside and outside the church, to a place where they tap into supernatural power or supernatural experiences in their own local church. However, I understand that some people may have good reason to be sceptical of prophecy in the context of the church, due to misuse. As a response, the book examines both the biblical justification for prophets as well as the outworking of the ministry. This is done at a personal and corporate level, so that the reader may recognize and develop the gift in both themselves and others. It is my hope that you will see clearly the benefits that this gifting brings for the benefit of the local church and those to whom we are entrusted to deliver the good news of Jesus Christ.

[2] See The Pilgrim Church by E.W Broadbent

2 Unwrapping the gift

The wonderful world of prophetic ministry is filled with controversy and people who act and speak in bizarre ways. Part of the problem is, of course, that they are trying to emulate those brave Old Testament prophets who lay naked on the floor, shaved off half their beards, wore sackcloth and ashes and generally acted in an anti-social ways to bring attention to an unpopular message. Over many years I have seen the credibility and value of prophecy undermined by those who insisted at the same time that their actions and words proved them to be 'the real thing'.

On one occasion a rather nasty email proclaimed that my long-term battle with cancer was the judgment of God for some imagined shortcoming in my life. Around the same time a lady came to me for prayer saying, "I am coming in great fear to see you." As we talked she revealed a previous experience with a prophet that had devastated her. She recalled: "The prophet said I had a secret sin and as a result God will give me breast cancer." The lady then added that the 'prophet' was unable to indicate to her the secret sin and had no solution to addressing this perceived failure. Imagine the fear and torment she lived under, anticipating that something she did not know about, had condemned her to this horrible affliction.

So how do we gain, maintain, and increase confidence in the prophetic ministry in the body of Christ? We shall see later that New Testament prophets were those who sought to bring life and direction to local churches in which they were fully integrated. They had no personal agenda designed to advance their own ministry, but rather served alongside others in leadership. Credibility was attained by recognizing the value of relationship and co-operation to see the church rise to its full potential.

When practiced correctly, prophetic ministry infuses the body of Christ with encouragement and strength. This is in sharp contrast to the desire of some of those calling themselves prophets whose mission is to destroy and bring judgment to a rebellious church.

"Let the prophet who has a dream tell his dream, but let the one who has my word speak it faithfully. For what has straw to do with grain?" declares the LORD. (Jeremiah 23: 28)

Straw is what is left after the grain is threshed out. Grain is the seed which can be used both for food to nourish and for planting to produce a harvest. A 'straw' word cannot produce anything positive whereas one of 'grain' has the power to create life. Those who want to speak such words must have the life of Christ actively at work in them. They must be worshippers, under authority and in right relationship with God and the church.

Prophetic people need to remember that they are channels of God's Spirit who are mostly dealing with the church, the Bride of Christ. This means being most careful in ministry since he is very jealous for his bride. A good example is a water pipe. If water is being pumped through a clean pipe you get clean water. But if there is dirt or some other contamination in the pipe, the quality of the water will be poor. So, keep your pipe clean!

Hearing God

As a child I lived in a small English village where life seemed somewhat idyllic. During those days of the Second World War we roved far and wide across the fields and into the woods. Most of our fathers were in the army or in war work and so we ranged freely under the care of our mothers. Occasionally the sound of a yodel or someone's name drifted in on the breeze to interrupt the latest activity and beckon one or more of our group to supper. Far away as we were, the voice could be clearly heard and carried a uniqueness that enabled each individual to distinguish their mother from anyone else's. Often any failure to respond would result in another child saying, "You had best go now: your mother is calling you". If the game was particularly absorbing, it was easy to block out the call. But sometimes the tone and intensity of the voice would indicate it wise to go immediately!

People are often curious about how it is possible to hear God speak. It is just like our mothers calling us when we were young: each of us hear the Father in unique and clear ways. In John 10: 27 we encounter Jesus being pestered by unbelieving Jews to plainly say whether he was the Christ or not. Rather than offer them a new and perhaps extraordinary insight, he replied it had already been revealed. It was just that they weren't his sheep; for those who were had both listened and believed. From this perspective it appears that all believers should be able to identify his voice. There is also a general sense in which God wants all believers to be conscious of him speaking to them.

Whether you turn to the right or to the left, your ears will hear a voice behind you, saying, "This is the way; walk in it." (Isaiah 30: 21)

In addition, the Bible includes accounts of those such as Isaiah himself, John the Baptist and Agabus, who were called to prophetic ministry and had a clarity of hearing that went beyond their own needs. They were raised up as spirit-anointed individuals to be equipping elements for the people of God, speaking direction and insight on his behalf. This has occurred since the early days of mankind. God has always had those who could specifically hear his voice and he continues to operate in this way.

God not only uses people to convey his messages, but also instructs directly. He came into the Garden of Eden in the cool of the day and said "Adam where are you?" – as if he didn't know exactly where Adam and Eve were! He told Noah to build an ark and Abraham not to fear. In Acts 8 we read of

Philip receiving instruction to approach a man in a chariot
while two chapters later Peter is warned not to call anything
impure that God has made clean.

What is prophetic ministry?

As Christians, it is both our birthright and privilege to enjoy an
intimate relationship with God. In 1 Peter 2: 9 we are identified
as a people chosen to declare his praises. Accordingly, all of
us are prophetic in our new nature and able to participate in
prophetic activity. This is generally manifested in the church
in four ways:

The Spirit of Prophecy

*Then the LORD came down in the cloud and spoke with him, and
he took of the Spirit that was on him and put the Spirit on the
seventy elders. When the Spirit rested on them, they prophesied,
but they did not do so again. However, two men, whose names
were Eldad and Medad, had remained in the camp. They were
listed among the elders, but did not go out to the Tent. Yet the
Spirit also rested on them, and they prophesied in the camp.*
(Numbers 11: 25-26)

There is significance here that those men who met with
Moses in the Tabernacle were themselves uniquely touched
by the Holy Spirit. They were not involved in prophecy in an
ongoing way, but responded to a singular anointing. There
are times throughout the Bible when the Holy Spirit falls in
an exceptional way in the midst of God's people. With this
corporate anointing there comes a sensitivity to his voice and
presence that allows those to prophesy who perhaps have
not previously even been able to recognize the voice of God
for themselves.

Hearing God is essential as we regularly gather in our local
churches. As the angel says in Revelation 19: 10: *"Worship God!
For the testimony of Jesus is the spirit of prophecy."* The evidence
of the presence of Jesus in our midst is characterized by the

release of the spirit of prophecy. Those who are present in the meeting step out into a free and unusual flow of the prophetic. It may be someone in a worship team who never usually does anything publicly apart from playing the guitar. Under a one-off anointing he begins to sing spontaneously a 'song of the Lord' from which flows a flood of anointing over the rest of the crowd. This person however, does not continue to do this – it was just for then.

I have been in meetings where children with no deep spiritual understanding of what prophecy entails suddenly begin to speak out a prophetic message that is totally beyond their own understanding and ability. This also releases such an anointing in the meeting that others are touched and begin to join in spontaneously. Once during a strongly anointed meeting, a musician began to play softly in a quiet time following worship. The tune grew more and more defined until it became obvious that he was actually prophesying on his instrument! All were impacted by this but to my knowledge he never did it again.

The gift of prophecy

Follow the way of love and eagerly desire spiritual gifts, especially the gift of prophecy. For anyone who speaks in a tongue does not speak to men but to God. Indeed, no one understands him; he utters mysteries with his spirit. But everyone who prophesies speaks to men for their strengthening, encouragement and comfort. (1 Corinthians 14: 1-3)

This describes for us the kind of prophetic manifestation that we expect to hear in the church on a regular basis as one of the nine gifts of the Holy Spirit. The gift is limited in its scope to ministering encouragement, motivation, comfort, and instruction in the context of the local church gathering.

Those who are moving in the gift of prophecy should focus on the corporate encouragement and motivational aspects of the gift rather than specific directional and correctional words to individuals or the congregation, since their role is limited. It is important to hear these brothers and sisters regularly so that the church is encouraged and strengthened.

A person operating solely in this gift will be alert during worship and prayer times. Their contributions will be revelatory in the sense that they will speak simply to general needs but also to specific things without addressing the individual. Thus people in a meeting may be suffering bereavement, heavy work pressure or doubt. The gifted person will stand up and prophesy generally into the relevant areas and bring comfort and encouragement.

I have frequently been impacted by people prophesying about the subject I am preaching on before I begin to speak. Sometimes they will actually read the scripture that I have chosen for focus. This gives me a special appreciation of the voice of God speaking in the Body. However, such messages are not generally crafted and directed specifically to individuals as a personal prophetic message, since their application goes beyond any one individual present.

Prophetic ministry

Two or three prophets should speak, and the others should weigh carefully what is said. And if a revelation comes to someone who is sitting down, the first speaker should stop. For you can all prophesy in turn so that everyone may be instructed and encouraged. (1 Corinthians 14: 29-31)

Sometimes God causes individuals to grow more prophetically than what they have so far experienced in using the gift of prophecy. This frequently occurs in churches where there are no prophets in the full sense and so a smaller-scale ministry develops. Often, such people will bring prophetic direction and insight in co-operation with the church leaders.

These verses seem to point to prophets but it is worth noting that there is reference to 'those who are sitting down'. This is a picture of those who are recognized as being prophetic but not counted among the prophets. It could be that such people would be in the process of becoming prophets but are as yet unready to take on the task. On the other hand they may never go further than the role of prophetic ministry, since it is not simply a matter of progression along the line to the goal of becoming a prophet.

In Acts 21: 9 Luke records a stay in Caesarea at the house of Philip the evangelist who had four daughters who prophesied. These young women were recognised by the local church as each possessing a prophetic gift that went beyond simply using the gift of prophecy. They appear to have held a reputation beyond that of the average church member who could prophesy. Interestingly, the next verse records the arrival of Agabus 'a prophet' – a title not applied to Philip's daughters.

One of the ways in which I like to train people with a prophetic ministry is to have them travel with me and prophesy as God gives them freedom to do so. This does not mean that they will 'graduate' as prophets but their insights will be enhanced by being alongside someone who does have that calling. They may be part of my team for several years but never develop in such a way. This is not a failing on their part, as the calling and gifting of God is not subject to the efforts of man.

The gift of a prophet

He who descended is the very one who ascended higher than all the heavens, in order to fill the whole universe. So Christ himself gave the apostles, the prophets, the evangelists, the pastors and teachers, to equip his people for works of service, so that the body of Christ may be built up. (Ephesians 4: 10-12)

The appointment of prophets is a divine act of initiation and not one that simply comes out of a number of years of service or achievement of an individual in the body of Christ. Neither is it an honorary title bestowed to bring a certain dignity to an individual or authority in a hierarchy. The coming of all the gifts mentioned above was purposeful in as much as they were actually each a part of the total ministry of Christ himself. They were designed to bring to the church reproductive power and building and authority. Thus, a prophet is a ministry gift of Christ who moves clearly in words of wisdom and knowledge and in most, if not all, the gifts of the Spirit.

When we look at prophets in the book of Acts, we see them as having more than prophetic insight. Agabus was able to perceive an upcoming famine and predict that Paul would be imprisoned in Jerusalem. Judas and Silas went from church to church bearing the Apostle's message about circumcision. They were received as those having authority and their message was acted on. Churches recognised them for what they were: senior leaders who, together with the other leadership positions, represented the overall rule of Christ as a gift for equipping and building them up.

It is therefore clear that having four kinds of expression of the prophetic does not mean that there is a ladder to climb beginning with the simplest and rising to a coronation at the top. While the other three are gifts of the Holy Spirit, the role of the prophet is one that is a gift of Jesus to the church.

The call of a prophet

In hearing God's voice it is important to understand that God is always the initiator and comes to speak to someone on his own terms and in his own time.

The LORD came and stood there, calling as at the other times, "Samuel! Samuel!" Then Samuel said, "Speak, for your servant is listening." (1 Samuel 3: 10)

Samuel was to be a prophet and God began the process by calling him just the way my mother did. He called several times and actually by name which underlines the importance of having a personal relationship with him. It is not merely a gift imparted by the laying on of someone's hands. In this relationship Samuel was to see himself not as a great person but simply as a servant. God was calling and Samuel was responding. Intimacy with God is the key that unlocks the ability to hear clearly.

Receiving a call may therefore not be a sudden event but rather a process involving responding to God in the only way we know how. Samuel's life reflected this as he came to a gradual realization. Eli played no small part in Samuel's development and usually those called to prophetic ministry will have others who point them in the right direction. The process of revelation is clearly shown emerging in the life of Jeremiah:

The word of the LORD came to me, saying, "Before I formed you in the womb I knew you, before you were born I set you apart; I appointed you as a prophet to the nations." "Ah, Sovereign LORD," I said, "I do not know how to speak; I am only a child. (Jeremiah 1: 4-6)

Firstly we see that God initiates the relationship through 'giving' the word and secondly he gives confirmation of the call – "I appointed you". Out of that relationship God began to show him things that were not of primary importance. Thus, we learn that prophetic people actually get taught by God to hear and see prophetically in a step-by-step procedure. Jeremiah's first interaction produced a vision that God affirmed as correct.

The word of the LORD came to me, "What do you see, Jeremiah?" "I see the branch of an almond tree," I replied. The LORD said to me, "You have seen correctly, for I am watching to see that my word is fulfilled." (Jeremiah 1: 11-12)

I remember in the early days of my ministry being asked to go to a small country church. The week before my visit I clearly saw a vision of a young child covered in allergy spots and I shared this with my wife. When the day came, we arrived at a small but quite formal Pentecostal church where

I was to conduct the whole service. After the first prayer and hymn I addressed the congregation and asked the mother with the suffering child to come forward.

Total silence and a sense of embarrassment stifled the air. The church nursery had long since been closed and filled with excess furniture. There was no adult under 50 in the whole building and certainly not a single child! Swiftly moving along, to cover my embarrassment, I worked my way through more worship and delivered a sermon. Afterwards, while eating lunch with a couple in the church, a young couple came through the garden gate accompanied by a three year old girl skipping behind them. The little girl was covered in a rash which the young mother explained was a result of some immunization in the previous week.

So what was happening? God was teaching me how to hear and see. He never told me I should make a public statement – that was my own idea. He was simply helping me gain confidence and in essence was saying that I had seen correctly. Sometime we can be so anxious to tell everyone that God is using and speaking through us but what he actually wants is for us simply to learn to have confidence which comes from confirmation.

My dear brothers, take note of this: Everyone should be quick to listen, slow to speak. (James 1: 19)

Part of learning to hear is also learning when to speak. In the classic story of Samuel and Eli, Samuel heard most clearly what God said about his mentor, but was reluctant to speak before God actually prompted him clearly. Finally, God does not speak to us based on our family pedigree, theological insight, or simply our desire to be 'someone' in the Kingdom of God. The call to the prophetic ministry and our ability to hear God are rooted in his sovereignty.

Amos answered Amaziah, *"I was neither a prophet nor a prophet's son, but I was a shepherd, and I also took care of sycamore-fig trees."* But the LORD took me from tending the flock and said to me, *"Go, prophesy to my people Israel."* (Amos 7: 14-15)

The key to Amos being called was the choice of God. In my own case I had no exposure to prophetic ministry or teaching and, like Amos, was not a prophet or the son of a prophet. But the Lord called me and demonstrated clearly that he had given me a gift which later developed into the call of a prophet to influence nations.

Confirmation

Those called to be prophets should know that God will not fail to recognize their call through others who themselves carry that ministry and who will bring impartation to release them to the task.

Surely the Sovereign LORD does nothing without revealing his plan to his servants the prophets. (Amos 3: 7)

Receiving recognition and confirmation is not to be a driving ambition but rather a quiet and humble waiting on God. I was serving as a leader of a flourishing church in Southern Alberta, with a modest but growing prophetic ministry around North America. During this time a team of prophets visited to minister into the heart of our church. Both leaders and those whom we believed to be called to various areas of ministry were present. At the close of one evening the team prayed with me and said, "God has called you to be a Prophet to the Nations".

Within weeks I had handed over responsibility for leadership of the church and was pursuing this calling. I never once had to telephone or write for the opportunity to share my gift and have continued like this for more than 40 years in prophetic ministry. Up until that time I had travelled with seasoned men, content to wait on the timing of God and not to manipulate the circumstances to my own program.

Receiving recognition from the church and its leaders is very important for enabling prophets to step into their role in the body of Christ.

For God, who was at work in the ministry of Peter as an apostle to the Jews, was also at work in my ministry as an apostle to the Gentiles. James, Peter and John, those reputed to be pillars, gave me and Barnabas the right hand of fellowship when they recognized the grace given to me. They agreed that we should go to the Gentiles, and they to the Jews. (Galatians 2: 8-9)

The apostolic role to be fulfilled by Paul was certainly exceptional. Yet even though he received his strong and convincing call by personal revelation, he still felt the need to go to those who were called 'pillars' and receive their blessing and release for his ministry. Judas, Silas and Agabus are the most frequently mentioned New Testament prophets. They too were acknowledged by their own local church leaders in Jerusalem and were willing to be sent elsewhere in the service of the body of Christ. This recognition gave them credibility with the churches that they ministered to.

Recognition however does come at a price. Acting as a lone ranger must give way to teamwork. Recognition means submitting to the leadership of other brothers and accepting responsibility. This is for the benefit of the church at home and in the broader context.

3 The Church needs prophets

The meeting had just finished when a young man approached me. He seemed sincere and obviously knew his Bible well, for a number of probing and penetrating questions followed. Speaking from a specific doctrinal position, he wanted to refute the existence of prophets and prophetic ministry in the church in modern days. Having begun my Christian walk in that same doctrinal mindset, I understood his need to disprove something which challenged his core understanding of the pattern of Christian revelation. Among other things, he wanted to know, "Why do we need prophets in our day?"

Many Christians are asking the same questions and looking for meaningful answers since there is a great hunger inside and outside the church for expressions of the supernatural. Some have recognized from the Scripture that there is to be an extraordinary outpouring of the Holy Spirit in the last days. On the day of Pentecost, a crowd from many different nations was startled to hear Galileans praising God in their own languages. Perhaps even more astonishing to them was Peter's explanation that this heralded the beginning of something announced by God through the prophet Joel at least four hundred years earlier. The time had finally arrived for God to pour out his Spirit on all people. Men and women, sons and daughters would prophesy and have divine dreams and visions.[3]

This has led to a belief in prophecy as a genuine manifestation of the Holy Spirit during the time before Christ returns. Such people are in good company, for when writing to the Corinthian church, Paul acknowledged a variety of spiritual gifts amongst them as they eagerly waited for this to happen.[4]

[3] Acts 2: 17-18
[4] 1 Corinthians 1: 7-8a

No doubt exists in my mind that God does indeed intend the church to access the full set of gifts right up until the day of Christ's physical return of to the earth. While this may be true, do we actually need prophets in the church today? Does God have a place for them in the church as we enter the critical days ahead or are they unnecessary on the basis that all can now prophesy, just as all can speak in tongues?

Prophets in the Bible

Prophets are depicted in the Bible during the days of restoration as those who were committed to stand alongside leaders and to help them in any way possible. One example comes from the book of Ezra when Zerubbabel and others were helped by the 'prophets of God' as they commenced the work of rebuilding the temple in Jerusalem.[5]

Further study reveals that whenever major change is intended, God uses all the resources at his disposal. In seeking to build churches firmly grounded on New Testament principles, we have no reason to believe that now would be any different. Clearly, the New Testament teaches us that Jesus gave the prophetic gift to the Church for ongoing use and equipping: *It was he who gave some to be apostles, some to be prophets, some to be evangelists, and some to be pastors and teachers to prepare God's people for works of service, so that the body of Christ may be built up.* (Ephesians 4: 11-12)

He does this in the same way in which prophets were raised up to help in the establishment of the city of Jerusalem in the Old Testament. After the resurrection of Christ, we see evidence of prophetic ministry as a continuing force in the emerging church. Antioch, in modern-day Turkey, was where the disciples were first called Christians. Birthed by believers scattered after a wave of persecution, they included both prophets and teachers whose roles were considered significant enough to have their names included in the book of Acts.

[5] Ezra 5: 2

In Acts 15: 32-34 we see that not only did this church benefit from such ministries within their ranks, but also from elsewhere. Judas and Silas are described not only as leaders but also as prophets, working in conjunction with other ministries in their own local church. Bearing a letter of instruction from the apostles and elders in Jerusalem, they encouraged and strengthened the Antioch church.

Thus a particular role of prophets is to help the church grow and equip believers to mature and persevere. Their gift is both very dear and important, not just to the leaders but also to the people. Paul wrote to the church in Ephesus that the prophetic ministry was one of the two foundational ministries that Christ had left for them to build with.[6]

The value to the New Testament church was not just in bringing greater resolve to those in need, but also in preparing people for works of ministry and bringing revelation of the future to leaders and people alike. On many occasions the purpose was to expose true condition, either collectively or individually.

In Revelation 2: 2 the Ephesian Church is commended for hard work and perseverance, for being intolerant of wicked men and exposing false apostles. In verse nine, the church in Smyrna receives encouragement that the Lord knows of their afflictions and poverty, yet he considers them rich. He even knows of the slander they endure from false Jews who are really a synagogue of Satan. Conversely, Revelation 3: 16 describes the Laodiceans as lukewarm and 'about to be spat out of the Lord's mouth'.

John's prophetic insight into each of the seven churches of Asia was invaluable to their future in God. They needed his perspective from outside in order to bring about personal and collective vision as well as change. This would result in correction without destruction and also bought confirmation to the leaders of the true state of their respective flocks.

[6] Ephesians 2: 20

Every local church has a need for such insight. This is not about gathering a profile through some sort of congregational survey but rather about gaining spiritual insight. Such valuable information helps churches to establish their identity – as they are not all called to be the same. None should be slavish reproductions of a 'Mother' church elsewhere but rather are unique expressions within the overall body of Christ, seeking to grow in their own purpose.

Individuals too are singled out in the same manner. In the Old Testament, we see Jacob calling his sons together and prophesying over each one, concerning character and destiny. Individually these men were to be the founders of distinctive tribes but collectively they would be known as the nation of Israel. Many years later, Samuel pronounces Saul and then David as King. This pattern continues into the New Testament. For instance in Acts 9: 15-16, the Lord commands a rather reluctant Ananias to heal Saul of Tarsus and tell him of his destiny as a chosen instrument to bear witness before Jews and Gentiles alike.

In our day we have not ceased to have the same needs as those who first received the Gospel message. Indeed, from the seventh generation of man, God saw the need for prophetic revelation and laid a foundation of hope and revelation for his people.

Enoch, the seventh from Adam, prophesied about these men: *"See, the Lord is coming with thousands upon thousands of his holy ones."* (Jude 14)

Winds of change

These are days of exciting change in the body of Christ. God is bringing the church into its own and is equipping it in ways that we have not seen for a long time. In my lifetime I have seen the recognition of both the Apostle and the Prophet in New Testament Churches become a reality. Back when I first came to know the Lord, it would have been almost heretical to even suggest that these ministries might soon become familiar sights on the landscape of life. So that span of time has seen some extraordinary and much-needed indeed.

In those days, there was recognition of the role of a Pastor. Those who fulfilled this role were normally kindly men who baptized your children, married those who wished for the blessing of God in their lives, and buried your grandfather at the end of his days on earth. As an additional duty they generally mowed the church lawns and tended the flower gardens.

The Evangelist was characterized as one who wore exceptional suits, gold watches and rings while telling stories of what happened in other churches in other cities. His presence in the church produced a momentary excitement but little long-term benefit.

The Teacher was the final recognized ministry or calling. Usually he was a somewhat grave person, with some knowledge of the Hebrew and Greek in which the original text of the Bible was written. From this person we would hear insights concerning the colour of the badger skins in the Tabernacle and other things so profound that they were never clearly understood. Frequently, we were either baffled, bored or both! This resulted in deciding that the speaker was 'deep', meaning we could not understand him, and he was therefore reckoned to be a Teacher!

At this juncture in history the Prophet and the Apostle had been confined to a place of non-existence by a prevailing theology that insisted that these were only gifts for the foundation of the church and not for present day Christianity.

Back in 1948, God began to bring a revelation to the church through the Latter Rain Revival which broke out in North Battleford in Northern Canada. The principles released in those days to the church were to reverberate around the earth and to be a catalyst for the release of the apostolic and prophetic ministries into the church once more.

Through the 1960s and the 1970s there was a resurgence of the teaching concerning modern day Apostles and Prophets as the Charismatic movement emerged on a global level. Men like the delightful and somewhat rascally Ern Baxter and his travelling companion James Watt particularly championed these truths in Canada and the USA.

Much controversy arose around the teachings of the Latter Rain Revival and many Orthodox Pentecostals chose to 'throw the baby out with the bathwater' because the challenge to change was not one they wanted to embrace. As a result the prophetic ministry was used as a 'whipping boy' to demonstrate the error of those brethren who embraced truths that God was restoring to the church. To this day there are strong groups of Classical Pentecostals who will not allow personal prophecy or directional prophecy of any kind in their Assemblies based on judgments made in the early 1950s.

In the 1980s and 1990s clear apostolic ministries were birthed and began to operate around the world. As in all times of the birth of new things there were aberrations and extremes, but there has come a maturing and grasping of a better understanding as people have walked out the call in their lives.

Unfortunately in the late 1990s a group of leaders tried to 'hijack the history' referred to above, and began to propagate a teaching tainted with personal kingdom building. Although divorcing themselves from other teachings on the ministry gifts they attempted to make themselves the successors to those who had paid a price and gone before them. Today there has been much confusion because of self proclaimed Apostles and Prophets. Nevertheless, the return and ministry of Apostles and Prophets in local churches and church streams [7] is becoming more of a reality.

---

[7] A "Church Stream" is a group of New Testament Churches which relate together. They have apostolic and prophetic oversight, but do not have a denominational hierarchy.

The return of the Prophet

The return of the Prophet to the scene has been a vital key to the growth and success of churches endeavouring to follow a New Testament pattern of operation. Where before they knew only poverty in mission and lacked purpose, today their experience is much different. I have been very privileged as a prophet to play a part in this change and have experienced great joy from being involved. I have lived long enough to see the outcome of many of my prophetic words in the lives of individuals and churches.

Seeing the intensity with which some of these churches have applied that word is illustrative of the fact that growth flows out of co-operation between church leaders and prophetic ministry. A while back I attended and ministered in a church in the North of England who met for convenience on a Sunday afternoon in an Anglican church. They had suffered spiritual abuse in the past and were now very suspicious of people who called themselves prophets. But they were at a stalemate in ministry and growth because of their place of meeting.

God was gracious to this lovely group of people as they struggled to express his grace in their needy community. During a meeting with them God gave me a prophetic word that he would give them a building. Specifically, this building would have previously been used as a medical facility or a sanatorium. It would be painted brown and unattractive in appearance! In addition God showed me that a certain man would resist their efforts to obtain such a property. So for ten years they investigated many properties seeking one that fitted the description. However, on several occasions they were frustrated by someone else buying the buildings that seemed to be just right.

Finally, they located what had been the theatre for a very large mental institution that had itself been converted to apartments. This building from the outside looked very

unattractive and the paint work was all in very dark brown.
In their negotiations they discovered that the developer was
a man who had bought out property after property that the
church had negotiated for! Today, what had been a struggling
group enjoys a beautiful building that could seat up to 900
people. They are a pulsating and growing church whose
testimony and message rings out into the nations. This church
used the prophetic word as a roadmap to get them out of
what could have been a dead end street.

The need for prophets in the church becomes even more
apparent as we consider these words of Paul:

*The weapons we fight with are not the weapons of the world. On
the contrary, they have divine power to demolish strongholds.*
(2 Corinthians 10: 4)

The clear indication on the nature of our weapons is that their
source is not derived from human wisdom. yet so many times
the church has sadly been totally bent out of shape by trying
to use methods and programs that do not have their roots in
the Holy Spirit. Rather they stem from the plans and purposes
of man-made strategy. People do not necessarily mean to
attempt things for God without his direction, but are simply
ignorant of the divine resources available to them alongside
the wisdom and work of their own hands.

Prophetic direction and intervention have an essential role
in breaking down strongholds and thereby helping us to
demolish the works of the enemy in our community. In
2 Kings 6: 1-6 we find a company of prophets telling Elisha that
their place of meeting with him was too small – it seems that
building problems are not a modern day phenomenon! So
they suggested each of them gathering some wood in order
to build a communal home. Elisha was requested to join them
and they made their way to the banks of the River Jordan. Of
course, not all axes are constructed perfectly and so as they
chopped down some trees, an iron axe-head flew loose into

the air only to plummet into the river. A cry of dismay then rang out from the man holding the shaft that remained. "Oh my lord!" he cried out to Elisha for the axe had been borrowed. Elisha responded by asking exactly where the axe had fallen. Next he cut a stick and threw it there. Within seconds the axe-head floated to the surface, much to the man's relief.

Here is a situation so typical of the thinking of many. A group of sincere men see a need to build and expand – the desire of many leaders. In undertaking the task they desire prophetic or supernatural involvement and confirmation. Asking Elisha to go with them was the measure of their felt need for such involvement with their project. And so they went about the building process with hardly a thought of Elisha until they realized that in the process they had lost something very valuable. The church has so often engaged in building either physically or spiritually with 'token' prophetic or supernatural presence. However, the point has soon been reached when they have appreciated the necessity of the supernatural to get the axe-head out of the water! It was Elisha's presence and contribution that added the supernatural element to the whole project. We are to war with prophetic words, supernatural weapons, that God has given us in the church, and not simply with our own naturally formed plans and weapons.

It has been my privilege to minister in many nations and for more than a decade I have travelled with teams to the beautiful island of Taiwan. Our teams have enjoyed so much the love and hospitality of the church in Taiwan over these years. We set out to work with three churches in that land and seen great success. Jeremy my son and I first visited a small group of around 30 young adults in the city of Taijung just before the turn of the new millennia. We sensed destiny over this church as we did over two other churches in the nation.

During our time we have worked with the leaders of the church and have prophesied vision, strategy and growth for them. This has seen the church increase very rapidly as not only the corporate body but also individual leaders become aware of personal destiny as they follow carefully the direction of the prophetic words they receive.

Today, the church has grown from the foundational 30 people to more than 2000 and is fast approaching 3000 in number. We have seen another miraculous situation like this in Taipei the capital, where another group have faithfully sought prophetic direction and then instituted its directions into their church life. This group has now seen growth to close to 2000 people.

These churches have drawn attention to themselves in the nation because of their growth and vitality. This comes from diligently applying the prophetic words they have received and not simply relegating them to a 'wasn't that nice' status and ignoring their direction for the church and its members.

The weapons we fight with are indeed supernatural and not merely the principles of a church growth manual. It is evident that projection of prophetic vision in the local church is a vital key to the success of that church in its community. Consider the words of Paul to his young disciple when urging him to persevere and grow in ministry:
Timothy, my son, I give you this instruction in keeping with the prophecies once made about you, so that by following them you may fight the good fight. (1 Timothy 1: 18)

The same principle must also apply corporately to the church. The emphasis is that we can fight with much confidence when we fight on the grounds of the prophetic word God has spoken to us. Every church does not have the same mission in a community. Merely attending conferences and applying principles, will be of no value unless we are doing it based on a Holy Spirit breathed prophetic foundation.

A while ago I tried for several years to plant a church in a community, basing my efforts on the pattern I had seen in the 'mother' church who had sent me out. We had astounding failure! The reason was because we were not building on a prophetic revelation for our church in our community but seeking to build 'on another man's foundation'. I am not speaking of some mystical revelation here but rather that very practical pointers come to us through prophetic words concerning the mission and involvement of our church in the community. I have had the joy of prophesying to churches about specific ways of outreach and unique venues for their work that have resulted in their having a profound impact on the community.

4 **Out from the wilderness**

For many people, the time after a meeting is a positive and relaxed affair. They can discuss and perhaps pray about what has just happened, meet new people or simply chat with friends about anything and everything. This isn't always my experience and once again I found myself warily eyeing an oncoming stranger. My suspicions proved correct for his speech revealed obviously distress and the need of an audience to express his feelings.

He was one of those 'polyester suit prophets' who dress formally on all occasions in attire not quite fitting with any current generation. Very pale and tight lipped he said, "I don't care if you are a New Testament prophet! I am an Old Testament prophet and I like to cut them off at the knees and leave them bleeding". The following words leapt out from my mouth: "The Scripture says that with the same measure that you use, it will be measured to you. Be it unto you according to your own word and faith". He left haughtily and hastily having 'delivered the word to me'. I am not sure what happened to him, but remain convinced that his approach is not the one Scripture would have us take.

There are not many people in church who I would consider as definitely normal. But come to that, there aren't many in the world either. Yet most of us appear as perfectly normal in the company of these 'strange prophets'. Sometimes it is not suits but long blue raincoats they appear in, surpassed only by the length of their beards. On other occasions it is not their clothing which places them way beyond the scope of normality but behaviour or manner of speech. Frequently these strange people who claim to be 'prophetic' are bizarre in a number of ways and seem to purposefully set out to be rejected in order to prove that they are in fact truly prophets. Modelling themselves on those in the Old Testament they shun people and claim to be totally infallible. It is therefore no wonder that such rejection of the ministry of Prophet has been prevalent for so long.

Perhaps fuelling the strange behaviour and rejection is no small amount of covenantal confusion in the church. In fact, we can be like the man at the circus who rides two horses at the same time with one foot on each! While some principles are similar between the two testaments, prophets and prophetic ministry are not the same. The church lives under a whole different covenant than the one that existed then. Old Testament prophets had the job of rebuking and correcting whole nations whereas now there is a new purpose. But first let us look at where we stand with regard to the two covenants.

The turning point

The cross of Christ is a turning point in history and changes the way God deals with men and nations and especially with his people. The roles and places of people before this pivotal event are totally changed by the sacrifice of Jesus. No longer is God trying to manifest himself to the earth through one nation but through a multinational body of men and women. Through these people he will show himself and accomplish his purposes on the earth.

Consequently, you are no longer foreigners and strangers, but fellow citizens with God's people and also members of his household. (Ephesians 2: 19)

Instead of a nation God is now manifesting his will and purpose through the church, a new nation that he has instituted and called out from every nation on the earth. Paul confirms this in Ephesians 3: 10-11 and goes on to say that is how God's manifold wisdom is now made known even to rulers and authorities in the heavenly realms.

Peter describes the inhabitants of this new nation as a chosen people and a royal priesthood. In calling us holy he recognises our being set apart as God's special possession.[8] Paul goes even further in 1 Corinthians 3: 16 by calling us God's temple in the midst of whom his Spirit dwells. Comparing the two covenants in 2 Corinthians 3: 7-8, Paul emphasises the glory of the latter over the former. For the former was temporary and to do with law but the latter is permanent and concerns the Spirit.

Along with a new nation and new temple, we also have a new high priest. Hebrews 4: 14-15 exhorts us to hold firmly to the faith we profess for in Jesus we have a great high priest who has ascended into heaven. He is able to empathise with our weaknesses as he has been tempted in every way just as we are – yet did not sin.

Ephesians reveals five ministries given by this new high priest to be foundational in building up the church and making it strong. These builders will make a solid base for others to build on as the verse says: ' ... *built on the foundation of the apostles and the prophets with Christ Jesus himself the Chief Cornerstone.'* (Ephesians 2: 20)

While it is true that God may still follow similar principles in choosing and developing men for prophetic ministry, the preparation is for an entirely different task to their Old Covenant counterparts.

A new ministry

As we look in the Bible we find ourselves challenged by the direct statements that God makes in connection to leadership in the church. Ephesians 4: 11 mentioned earlier tells us that God gave the church five ministry gifts which include both Prophet and Apostle. Many have had no difficulty in identifying Pastors, Teachers and Evangelists but have balked at the suggestion that the other two might still exist.

[8] 1 Peter 2: 9

In the original language however this verse is in the continuous tense and therefore gives us no reason to believe that God has ever ceased to provide these gifts as a manifestation of the ministry of Jesus to his Church. Looking at the verse, if you have no problem with a pastor, teacher or evangelist in the church, then there is equally no reason to have an issue with Jesus continuing to place gifts of apostles and prophets also. However, for many years the church has existed and limped along with only a three-pronged ministry of pastors, teachers and evangelists. The other two have either been forcefully rejected or simply neglected out of ignorance. The significance of either office has not been understood or overwhelmed by leaders own understanding of the titles involved.

The Prophet receives even worse press than that of the Apostle. People are mostly willing to look in the books of Acts and the Epistles for role models of the other four ministries but when it comes to seeking out prophets, they invariably cite Elijah and Jeremiah as the prototype and role models of the prophetic ministry.

It is important to understand that 'Prophet', like 'Elder', is a descriptive word that had a meaning under the old covenant which is not carried through intact to the new and thus also is not carried through into the life of the church. For example the Elder was a man of mature years honoured for his age and experience, yet in contrast when writing to Timothy, a new covenant Elder, Paul wrote "don't let anyone despise your youth". The new version of Elder is one who exercises government and disciplinary correction in concert with other elders in the local church. Likewise the Prophet was a lone voice of correction and discipline, yet in the New Testament there is no indication of this role.

Thus in the New Covenant we now have the following elements:

A New High Priest	Jesus himself
A New Priesthood	Every believer
A New Nation	The Church where there is neither Greek nor Jew
A New Temple	Composed of believers who are 'lively stones'
A New Ministry	Based on the Five Aspects of Christ's own ministry on Earth

If we want to understand the role of New Testament prophets, then a good starting place is Jesus himself.

Jesus the Prophet

Jesus himself was a prophet and this was readily acknowledged by many that encountered him. In Matthew 21: 11 as Jesus entered Jerusalem on a donkey, large crowds flung their cloaks and spread branches on the road before him. Sensing the excitement, the inhabitants of Jerusalem asked who they were doing this for and the crowds answered emphatically, "This is Jesus, the prophet from Nazareth in Galilee."

Jesus is the pattern for New Testament prophets, and those he called to prophetic ministry after his resurrection will bear in their lives the same marks and calling. Note he is referred to here as "Jesus the prophet", not "Jesus a prophet" as is befitting of the one who sets the standard for all others to follow.

However, on occasion Jesus did behave in a similar way to the prophets who appeared before him. Like Moses, David and Jonah he displayed righteous anger and turned over the tables of the money changers in the temple grounds. As Jeremiah cried many anguished tears because of the sins of the people and spoke of forthcoming judgments, so Jesus wept over Jerusalem and prophesied judgment on the city for rejecting the peace that was offered them.

While these can be regarded as necessary and in some respects part of the transition from one covenant to another, they also signify that there are still aspects of judgment included in the New Testament ministry. According to the book of Hebrews, the new elements supersede the former covenant which is only a 'shadow or type' of what should come after and what we as new covenant believers should now be enjoying.

The law is only a shadow of the good things that are coming – not the realities themselves. For this reason it can never, by the same sacrifices repeated endlessly year after year, make perfect those who draw near to worship. (Hebrews 10: 1)

In a previous verse the new covenant is described as making the old one obsolete and due to vanish.[9] Last in the line came John the Baptist and his comment concerning Jesus the author of the new order was, "He must increase and I must decrease". We could say that John was actually the bridge or transitional prophet between two covenants. His own testimony concerning Jesus' ministry and place is a confirmation of a new line of prophetic ministry flowing from Jesus himself.

Reconciliation

Jesus truly desired to bring reconciliation and restoration. Rather than heed the warnings brought by some Pharisees to avoid Herod's murderous intentions, he pressed on undeterred towards Jerusalem. The agony of arrest and crucifixion lay ahead yet his concern was for the very people who would soon be clamouring for his death.

"O Jerusalem, Jerusalem, you who kill the prophets and stone those sent to you, how often I have longed to gather your children together, as a hen gathers her chicks under her wings, but you were not willing!" (Luke 13: 34)

[9] Hebrews 8: 13

In the town of Nain, Jesus is found (not for the first time) building up and consoling those in need of ministry.[10] At the town gate he encounters a corpse being carried out by a large crowd of mourners. The grief is particularly heavy upon the mother who has lost her only son for she is a widow. Now there is no one to live for or to look after her. Feeling the agony within her heart as though it was his, he stares deeply into eyes red with torment and says softly, "don't cry".

Perhaps the crowd goes silent as he touches the coffin and the men carrying it stand still. Some will have already seen him break the bounds of normality and become excited with anticipation while others are simply puzzled. Yet all eyes fix upon him and all suddenly gasp with awe as upon his command the dead son stirs, sits up and begins to talk.

Loud celebrations break out, praising God and proclaiming a great prophet has truly appeared among them. Jesus meanwhile is presenting the young man to his mother and breathing in her relief. Sudden grief to sudden joy. This is what intoxicates him, this is his food and drink, a foretaste of the joy that lays waiting at the cross. For such things no pain seems too great to bear.

John 8: 3-11 finds Jesus with another large crowd, but this time in the temple courts. Jealous of his popularity and desperate to prove their superior learning, the teachers of the law and the Pharisees interrupted with a 'certain winner'. Associating with sinners was Jesus' trademark and not something according to them that righteous people should do. Moreover he had shown mercy and compassion and even forgiven some their sins against God. Only God could do this, so who was he? What was more, the law clearly cried out punishment for such crimes. Nasty punishments like stoning women guilty of committing adultery.

[10] Luke 7: 11-16

They dragged her in ruthlessly. Caught in the very act, no one could protest her innocence, so Jesus had to condemn her or contradict the law in full view of all who were present. What would you do? Jesus being who he was knew straight away of her guilt. Maybe the strange response of writing on the ground was designed to diffuse the situation or buy him time. More probably it was to allow the Holy Spirit to bring conviction to everyone present.

Questions kept bearing down upon him as he wrote with his finger. Finally he straightened up and replied, *"If any one of you is without sin, let him be the first to throw a stone at her."* Then he continued silently as before, writing words that can only be guessed. One at a time they moved away, the older and wiser ones first until all were gone. Now it was just the woman and Jesus. Did he let her off the hook? Yes and no. One day he would bear her punishment but she had to leave her life of sin. And the reason was so that reconciliation could happen between her and God.

Building the church, predicting the future

Jesus demonstrated the ability to accurately predict his own future and that of others. In Luke 18: 31-33 he tells his main disciples that everything predicted about him by the prophets would happen when they reached Jerusalem. This included being mocked, insulted, spat upon, flogged and killed. But also that he would rise again.

On occasion he spoke to the disciples of their individual destinies. How astonished Simon Peter must have been to hear his life described as a rock on which the church would be built.[11] What's more the gates of Hades would not overcome it. Luke 18: 31-33 reveals that Satan had asked permission to sift Peter as happens to wheat. But Jesus had already intervened and prayed so that his faith would ultimately stand the test. Interestingly, Jesus' primary concern is not to

[11] Matt 16: 18

do with Peter's failure but the need for him to strengthen his brothers once he had recovered.

Passion and purpose in building the church was very much part of Jesus' ministry and a pattern that developed in those who followed him as prophets. Barnabas was described as a great blessing to individuals and churches in the infant days of the Church. Scholars tell us that his name in the original language means 'son of prophecy' or 'son of encouragement'. The combination of these two things tell us the kind of people we should expect to be involved in New Testament church prophecy.

5 What do New Testament prophets do?

I have so much enjoyed my exposure to the churches in Germany and delighted in the laughter and fellowship enjoyed with so many. In the Hunsruck area of Germany I spent a short time with a pastor seeking to develop a strategy for growth. One day he took me on a tour of three towns in the area. In each of them we prayed that God would give unique revelation and in particular their readiness to receive the Gospel.

In one town I sensed the existence of a 'remnant of believers' waiting for a church to begin. During our debriefing at the end of the day he told me that the main purpose of the tour was to gain confirmation as to where to plant a new church. In the very town I had identified the remnant, his own local church had a strong prayer group meeting. My discernment now gave him the confidence that this town was indeed the right place to pioneer. Today there is a church planted there that I have had the privilege of preaching to and ministering into its strategy and vision.

Laying foundations for growth

Meeting and praying with leaders and attempting to help them has always proved to be a valuable and often uplifting experience. In East Anglia in the UK where I have worked for many years with leaders of the Newfontiers stream, I have been included in the prayer and discussion of those involved in planting new churches and strengthening existing ones. On many occasions we have had clear revelation as to strategy and method of approach as well as clear descriptive pictures of buildings and facilities that they can use to further the cause of the Kingdom in their communities.

To one group I discerned that God wanted them to have a building that had been paid for by Christians of another generation. In the picture I saw the building with a roof but no floor. In addition God showed me that it had to do with a wall or a gate and that it was somehow connected to fish!!

Searching diligently they eventually discovered a de-commissioned Anglican church. Peering through the windows they saw only a roof and a simple dirt floor. When approaching the owners they found reluctance to let the building again be used for worship, but agreed to do so for a modest rent. As they went through the deeds and process of buying they discovered that the original name of the building was Fishergate Church!

This encouraged them to value even more the usefulness of prophetic insight. After further similar direction, they moved on to a new and more strategic location and now have a dynamic ministry to students and two campuses in the city from which they are reaching out and claiming kingdom ground.

Some leaders have almost totally neglected the ministry of the prophet when it comes to laying the foundations of local churches. Their vision is frequently based on demographics and population survey and does not include what God has provided to help in this most important of tasks. In 1 Corinthians 12: 28 we read:

And in the church God has appointed first of all apostles, second prophets, third teachers, then workers of miracles, also those having gifts of healing, those able to help others, those with gifts of administration, and those speaking in different kinds of tongues.

Prophetic ministry will help build good foundations and enable growth. However, it must be recognized in order to function since this is the first step to actually releasing and using the gift in the church. Without recognition individuals will be unable to function to their potential in God and the church will be spiritually impoverished.

As such, prophets should be involved from the beginning. An Old Testament shadow of this principle is demonstrated in the story of Ezra and his companions as they set out to rebuild the house of God.

Now Haggai the prophet and Zechariah the prophet, a descendant of Iddo, prophesied to the Jews in Judah and Jerusalem in the name of the God of Israel, who was over them. Then Zerubbabel son of Shealtiel and Jeshua son of Jozadak set to work to rebuild the house of God in Jerusalem. And the prophets of God were with them, helping them. (Ezra 5: 1-2)

Churches without a prophetic vision invite their members to run unrestrained after their own vision. Imagine what sort of temple might have arisen without direction! No wonder so many churches become shipwrecked by falling into factions of disagreement and wandering off in different directions. As Proverbs 29: 18 says 'Where there is no revelation, the people cast off restraint; but blessed is he who keeps the law.'

In Ephesians 4: 13-14, Paul clearly saw the need to reach unity in the faith and become mature in Christ. Anything less would result in being 'tossed back and forth by the waves, and blown here and there by every wind of teaching and by the cunning and craftiness of men in their deceitful scheming.' But this maturing is not simply a matter of good teaching and instruction. Prophetic ministry will challenge a church to change and will expand the vision and build faith in the hearts of the hearers. Thus, maturing churches will not simply be doctrinally stable but also be motivated supernaturally to personal and corporate growth by giving heed to the prophetic voices that God sends them.

Assigning the workers

Frequently a call to ministry is delivered to people through the prophetic voice. Their lives are impacted as they become conscious of a God-given destiny. Such calling enables them to stand firm in situations of great pressure and difficulty when others would give up and go home.

The church in Antioch emerged from the work of men who themselves were used to distressing times. After the stoning of Stephen a great persecution broke out that saw many believers displaced from their homes. Some of them reached Antioch in Syria, an important city of over 500,000 inhabitants and around 300 miles away from Jerusalem. As they faithfully shared the good news, God blessed them and a great number of people became believers.

Helping this new church to flourish were both prophets and teachers including Barnabas and Saul (also called Paul). During a time of worship and fasting, the Holy Spirit commanded them to set apart Barnabas and Saul for the work to which they were called.[12] Here we see that God was doing definitely the calling but the church, through these prophets and teachers, was doing the separating.

There was no single person declaring a divine calling to a certain ministry either by their own authority or by that of another and particularly not from outside the context of the local church. Sometimes the case of David in the Old Testament, anointed by the prophet Samuel, is cited for credibility. However ,as already explained the New Testament pattern of operation is different. It involves church leaders much like – but not confined to – the Antioch team of prophets and teachers who sought God on behalf of Paul and Barnabas.

Timothy certainly had this plural experience as he was told by Paul to fight the good fight by following the prophecies made about him.[13] and not to neglect his gift, given to him through a prophetic message by the church elders.[14]

[12] Acts 13: 1-3
[13] 1 Tim 1: 18
[14] 1 Tim 4: 14

Obviously, Paul an Apostle, was involved with them in this matter because we also read in the same letter:

For this reason I remind you to fan into flame the gift of God which is in you through the laying on of my hands. (2 Timothy 1: 6)

Prophetic ministry is a vital part of the building process as it identifies the individual stones and where they fit in the purpose and plan of God in local churches. Sometimes they see potential in some that others would not recognize. After all, none are called to be inactive.

You also, like living stones, are being built into a spiritual house to be a holy priesthood, offering spiritual sacrifices acceptable to God through Jesus Christ. (1 Peter 2: 5)

The key here is that the house being built is a spiritual one and more than just a mere recognition of natural talents gifts and abilities is required.

Predicting the future

Recent years have seen much 'wildfire' prophecy about future events that can neither be checked nor acted upon. Other so-called prophecies meanwhile are actually quite predictable. For instance a prophetic word frequently surfaces concerning California falling into the sea. Charismatic Christians living comfortably elsewhere are fascinated by this thought, although Californians are not so enthusiastic! However, it is a well known fact that a fault line exists through California that could cause a major earthquake at some time in history.

Another prophecy describing a 'claw' being destroyed in the heavenly realms, received much attention on Christian television. It would imminently result in a 'great release' occurring on the earth. Yet as we eagerly watched on TV, nothing specific accompanied the message and it remained cloaked in mystery. All that could be fathomed was a probable removal of sin would be removed and Jesus himself returning. More recently, an extravagant prophetic word was repeated in certain meetings in the USA. It proclaimed that Jesus would actually return right there in the meetings that were going on in a 'revival atmosphere' and that they would be the scene of the second coming.

Prophecy is not needed to tell us that Jesus will come again, for the Bible assures us of this. We are also told that no one knows the day or the hour and that if anyone says it will be in a particular place, we shouldn't believe them.[15] How dearly I wish those Scriptures had been considered before either of those two 'prophecies' had been put forth.

When predictions do occur from true New Testament prophets they can be considered carefully and acted upon. My father would frequently say to me in other contexts, 'forewarned is forearmed'. The point being that when we know what is happening we can prepare in practical ways for it. Prophecy from a trusted source will hopefully see a church ready to give both resource and effort to help in what is to come. When this occurs, credibility will be given to the ministry both inside and outside the church.

The arrival of Agabus and his prophetic team at the Antioch church was accompanied by specific prophetic revelation of future events:
During this time some prophets came down from Jerusalem to Antioch. One of them, named Agabus, stood up and through the Spirit predicted that a severe famine would spread over the entire Roman world. (This happened during the reign of Claudius.) The disciples, each according to his ability, decided to provide help for the brothers living in Judea. This they did, sending their gift to the elders by Barnabas and Saul. (Acts 11: 27-30)

This was no vague apocalyptic prophecy concerning the distant future, but specific revelation of something the church could practically address. The response was instantaneous and the passage reveals that the event prophesied actually happened. This gave the infant church great confidence in the Prophets and their ability to speak concerning events of national or international impact.

During a gathering of pastors in Minnesota many years ago, God gave me a clear vision of the total destruction of the Berlin wall. At the time there were absolutely no evidence or reason to suggest that this might happen at all. Feeling somewhat abashed I gave the prophetic word and felt that somehow I was now at the point of being a false prophet. There was warm agreement from those present that this was a word from God. It was more than eight years later when I saw with my own eyes the Berlin Wall crashing to the ground on my television, and thanked God that my ministry was saved after all. I have wondered what practical steps could or should have been taken.

Some years before September 11th 2001 when passenger airplanes were flown into the Twin Towers and the Pentagon, I received a prophetic word in a public meeting in Montana. I announced that 'tentacles of fear' were coming out of the heart of the Middle East and would begin to penetrate American heartland. This would cause Americans to see things happening in their own country that previously they had only seen happening in battle-torn countries. I took no pleasure in the fact that people called to remind me of this prophecy following both the World Trade Centre bombing and the events of '9/11'. I have similar feelings to those regarding the Berlin Wall about what practical steps could or should have been taken.

Neither of these major predictions are mentioned in order to elevate myself, but rather to point out that prophetic ministry can and should have the ability to see and prophesy clearly future events and allow the church the opportunity to prepare practically for it. We have been plagued by too much vague prophecy that is fulfilled somewhere in the heavenly realms but has no practical outcome here on earth.

Strengthening and encouraging

Many so-called prophets may be evangelists who are angry at
the Church and looking for a channel to express their anger,.
Unsurprisingly the eventual outcome is destructive and
condemnatory prophecy. This was certainly a valid ministry of
the Old Testament prophet who did not exist in the context of
local church life and was called to bring correction as well as
direction to a whole nation.

However, there is no place in the New Testament for the
prophet being the chief agent of correction and discipline in
the local church. In the New Testament Church, discipline and
correction become the work of the local church elders, who are
called specifically to watch over the church and its discipline.
New Testament prophets are called to encourage and to
strengthen the church, not to tear it down and destroy it.

*Everyone who prophesies speaks to men for their strengthening,
encouragement and comfort.* (1 Corinthians 14: 3)

In Acts 15: 27 we read that Judas and Silas were sent as
representatives of the church in Jerusalem to deliver the
decision of the leaders to the people at Antioch concerning
Gentile believers. They were both prophets who 'said much to
encourage and strengthen the brothers.' When coming into a
receptive atmosphere, as they did, there is the chemistry for
many things to happen.

*Early in the morning they left for the Desert of Tekoa. As they
set out, Jehoshaphat stood and said, "Listen to me, Judah and
people of Jerusalem! Have faith in the LORD your God and
you will be upheld; have faith in his prophets and you will be
successful."* (2 Chronicles 20: 20)

Opportunity abounds to release and build faith in the hearts
of whole congregations when Prophets are accepted as
speaking on behalf of God. Faith arises from embracing
what is said, resulting in the Holy Spirit opening hearts and

sometimes dramatic things happening. People are rarely changed or saved simply by intellectual decision-making.

But if an unbeliever or someone who does not understand comes in while everybody is prophesying, he will be convinced by all that he is a sinner and will be judged by all, and the secrets of his heart will be laid bare. So he will fall down and worship God, exclaiming, "God is really among you!" (1 Corinthians 14: 24-25)

Bringing to repentance and faith

Part of the mission of the church is that every ministry should have an evangelistic ingredient. Prophets are no exception and much of their revelatory ministry is to touch the lives of unbelievers and lead them to Christ. Although often uninterested and unimpressed by our theology, many are nevertheless still searching for meaning beyond the emptiness of evolution and atheism.

In his own time Jesus noted in Matthew 16: 4 how the people still looked for a miraculous sign even though they were wicked and adulterous. Often he prophesied openly in public places in the presence of both followers and opponents. For instance in Matthew 23: 34-38 he tells the gathered crowd what they will do to the prophets, wise men and teachers sent after him. Some would be killed and crucified while others they would flog in the synagogues and pursue ruthlessly from town to town.

This is indeed what happened and perhaps some remembered his words and even repented of their crime. For Jesus also told them of the dreadful consequence that would follow: a falling upon them of all the innocent blood shed by the prophets, from Abel to Zechariah, resulting in the destruction of the Temple in Jerusalem. Josephus reports that such was the hatred of the Roman soldiers for the Jews, that when they advanced upon the Temple in around AD70, they ignored their commander and burnt it to the ground.

So many Jews, most of whom were peaceful citizens, were butchered in the process that their blood ran like stream down the steps. Those slain at the top slipped to the bottom creating a heap of corpses about the altar.[16]

The prophetic ministry has a dynamic part to play in the field of evangelism both in and outside of church family meetings. Sadly, so many prophets have isolated themselves from both the church and the world and no longer have a relevant message to bring to either. The Apostle Paul in contrast was always finding new settings for ministry, in the midst of idols, in synagogues and by riversides to proclaim the good news and give accompanying miraculous signs.

Today God has sent a new manifestation of that same spirit to the church. God is getting the church out into the world where meetings are being held anywhere from pubs to ancient buildings. In a series of meetings I was holding in the Midwest of the USA the chosen venue was a local university. On my first night the room was packed with students, both believers and unbelievers. After some worship the stage was mine. I was just about to stand up when a church leader tugged on my shirt and said "You had better do well". In response to my questioning look he continued, "Last week there was a New Age guy here doing meetings. He floated a large heavy table around the room."

This was quite a launching pad! For the next four nights we received extraordinary revelations about the lives of those present and as we shared, people came to know Jesus for themselves.

Working in teams

The New Testament prophets were almost always in teams. Unlike their Old Testament counterparts who thrived in solitude and loneliness, those in the book of Acts were

[16] Duruy, Victor, History of Rome vol. V (1883)

conscious of the need to move in a group as Jesus had done with his own disciples.

Learning to flow with other prophets can be very difficult for those who have been raised in the environment where they are considered to exclusively be the main person. I have worked with some who could not adjust to team-working in prophetic ministry. They feel they must always be the first to prophesy for individual candidates and the church. Those who are watching find it both embarrassing and amusing to observe such a person trying to operate in a team context.

Paul's teaching in 1 Corinthians 14: 29 speaks of prophets working in a plural context. Proverbs 11: 14 sensibly says that *"For lack of guidance a nation falls, but many advisers make victory sure."* The translation in the King James version puts it as "in the multitude of counsellors there is safety".

Again and again the book of Acts emphasizes the place of team in every aspect of church life and government. In Acts 11: 27-28 and 21: 10 we find mention of Agabus and those travelling with him. In Acts 15: 32 Judas and Silas are seen to be working together. Thus, it is clearly illustrated that these men sought to bring their message in the context of team rather than as individuals, giving safety and authenticity to those who heard.

Finally, as we stress the importance and value of prophetic ministry today, there is another vital aspect to consider. In days of stress and pressure the church needs a present revelatory word from God. We need to know that God is still speaking to his church and is not silent.

There is no greater word of revelation than the Bible itself:

And we have the word of the prophets made more certain, and you will do well to pay attention to it, as to a light shining in a dark place, until the day dawns and the morning star rises in your hearts. Above all, you must understand that no prophecy of

Scripture came about by the prophet's own interpretation.
For prophecy never had its origin in the will of man, but men
spoke from God as they were carried along by the Holy Spirit.
(2 Peter 1: 19-21)

The church must have a directive and revelatory word from
God in each generation. Not one that contradicts or goes
against the spirit of the written word but one that directs
believers to the current concern and emphasis of God in
their own generation. Future events will drive the church to
needing specific direction from God. This 'present word' must
come from the mouth of seasoned and proven prophetic
ministries and can be vital for the protection and direction
of the local church.

6 Prophetic churches

The evening had gone well as far as I was concerned. The people were now dispersing and I was thinking of leaving when another memorable experience occurred. I should have noted the familiar signs of a few individuals hanging around, engaging in conversation and occasionally pausing to 'give me the eye'. But they say that fools never learn and sure enough, now standing as I was on my own, over they came.

On this occasion it was a very earnest lady and a couple of companions who approached with a smile. "Thank you for your word tonight! We are used to this kind of teaching because we come from a prophetic church". Well this seemed positive enough and so, still having a few minutes to spare, I engaged them in conversation thinking it might be interesting. My request for a description of their church yielded the following information:

They engaged in 24/7 prayer and never closed their doors. In addition, special meetings frequently occurred and always led by prominent and well known 'international prophetic teachers'. Their conferences were well attended and people came from far and wide. They attracted musicians, artists, and those who enjoyed the excitement attached to their activities. The meetings yielded considerable predictions of how their city would experience an incredible revival and how the enemies of Christ around the world would be suddenly cast down. All this was shared with enthusiasm and apparently without any need for any of the predictions to have a practical outcome.

Many people in North America might describe a prophetic church in that way. In my travels I have come across many versions. The description is usually applied to those fellowships who are a little more esoteric or mysterious than other churches and who major on 'catching the next wave of the Holy Spirit' and gaining mystic interpretations of Old Testament Scripture. They can display a tendency to harp back to the Old Testament style of worship and frequently struggle with covenantal schizophrenia, seeking to embrace law and grace at the same time.

So what are prophetic churches and does the Bible lead us to understand that they should really exist? The most clear vision of operating in the full sphere of prophetic ministry is seen in the principal churches of Jerusalem and Antioch. Both had well-developed prophetic elements that were clearly recognized and relied upon. They stand in stark contrast to the many 'Prophetic Churches' of today who are simply led by a charismatic personality with little regard for the input or insight of those around him. In fact the questioning of any direction he brings is immediately countered with the equivalent of 'don't lift your hand against the Lords anointed!'

Today in the Western world, there are basically three kinds of churches which align with the words of our Lord:

"I am the way and the truth and the life. No-one comes to the Father except through me." (John 14: 6)

We see:

- Way churches which are primarily evangelistic in their orientation.
- Truth churches which have a heavy focus on teaching and discipleship.
- Life churches which are characterised by the prophetic and gifts of the Holy Spirit.

Since Jesus characterized Himself as being all three, it tells us we should not be striving to build any one of the three to the exclusion of the other two. Similarly, we need to be seeking for a church with a balanced expression of the prophetic ministry alongside the other aspects of New Testament life.

To view this in action we need to look at the early church patterns, where we can see the place prophetic ministry played in their overall experience of church life. Both Antioch and Jerusalem were churches of apostles and elders and obviously produced prophets who actively influenced well beyond their neighbourhood. The Antioch church particularly gives us a clear picture of what it means to be fully-developed and contained the following elements that need reproducing in our day:

Spirit and Word

In the church at Antioch there were prophets and teachers. (Acts 13: 1)

The church had a vision which included the Spirit and the Word along with the government and gift ministries to support it. To some a prophetic church would be one where, in their view of the book of 1 Corinthians, 'everyone can prophesy one by one' without any discrimination. There would be a regular cacophony, a cornucopia of prophetic expression.

Yet prophetic ministry was not the be all and end all of church life. Teachers as well as prophets were prominent in Antioch for the call of the Lord was not just to revelation but also to solid down-to-earth teaching about how to live as well as what to expect from the presence of the Holy Spirit.

These prophets were in the church. They had the same heartbeat as the teachers and their vision was harnessed together to build a church that would impact the whole of Asia and most of the world of that day. This church was one that embraced Jew, Gentile, and black and white. Amongst those named was Simeon whose very name suggests he was a man of colour and then Lucius, a Gentile name, along with Manaen raised in the home of Herod the Tetrarch and Paul himself, the Pharisee of Pharisees. This was an embracing prophetic congregation that encompassed culture and race with apparent ease. They set an incredible example of what it means to be a team and operate under the anointing of the Holy Spirit as a united voice.

Not only this, but there were obviously Apostles present. Paul and his companions were a full blown Apostolic team! There can be no strong prophetic church unless it is founded equally strongly on the teaching of the Bible. Without the guideposts of the Scripture expounded by anointed teachers there can be no safe ministering of the prophetic ministry in the local church.

Churches and movements that attempt to operate prophetic ministry outside the guidelines of solid biblical teaching end up leading their followers into deception from which it is hard to recover. At the same time churches with dynamic teaching ministry can sometimes totally dry up spiritually due to a total lack of the supernatural which is also needed in their daily lives.

Credibility

Do not put out the Spirit's fire; do not treat prophecies with contempt. Test everything. Hold on to the good
(1 Thessalonians 5: 19-21)

The congregation is most conscious of the attitude of their leaders towards everything in the prophetic ministry. I went to a church for many years and prophesied significant things to them. Their leader gave lip-service to the prophetic ministry and never took it seriously. This resulted in an attitude of contempt toward the personal prophecies that came over individuals and corporately in the church.

When prophetic ministry is welcomed there is a rising of faith in the hearts of individuals and a growth of the corporate body. At Antioch there was a true understanding of the value of what they were receiving. I believe that Agabus was a foundational prophet for them and they received him as such. He seems to have visited them quite often and had a significant effect when he did. This is because he was received for what and who he was. In Matthew 10: 41 we read:

Anyone who receives a prophet because he is a prophet will receive a prophet's reward, and anyone who receives a righteous man because he is a righteous man will receive a righteous man's reward. (Matthew 10: 41)

Great blessing awaits churches who receive regular prophetic input and have great confidence in those who come to them. When Elisha was received in the home of the Shunammite woman it resulted in fertility, life and a manifestation of the miracle power of God. A prophetic word is therefore not to be taken lightly and certainly not ignored. It is not even to be rationalized but rather to be worked through. In short something must be done about it.

While they were worshipping the Lord and fasting, the Holy Spirit said, "Set apart for me Barnabas and Saul for the work to which I have called them." So after they had fasted and prayed, they placed their hands on them and sent them off. (Acts 13: 2-3)

Prophetic-oriented churches pray meditatively and reflect upon the words they receive and give credibility to those words by actually acting on them.

Direction

Paul and his companions travelled throughout the region of Phrygia and Galatia, having been kept by the Holy Spirit from preaching the word in the province of Asia. When they came to the border of Mysia, they tried to enter Bithynia, but the Spirit of Jesus would not allow them to. So they passed by Mysia and went down to Troas. During the night Paul had a vision of a man of Macedonia standing and begging him, "Come over to Macedonia and help us." After Paul had seen the vision, we got ready at once to leave for Macedonia, concluding that God had called us to preach the gospel to them. (Acts 16: 6-10)

Not only did the Antioch church give credibility to prophetic ministry but it became part of their strategy to deploy people and resources. Logically it made little sense to send Paul and Barnabas away when they were so obviously valuable there, but it was the Holy Spirit who commanded them to do so. Being an obedient and releasing church, they did what was contrary to their natural minds and released Paul and his team to the new direction of the Spirit. Nurtured as they were in the prophetic atmosphere of Antioch, this team were greatly influenced by prophetic revelation in their strategy. They came from a church where the prophetic was an ordinary and valuable part in determining direction.

Many years ago, I led a successful New Testament church that was growing strongly in Southern Alberta. We were visited by a team of prophets for a three day intensive prophetic summit. One night there was a consensus amongst the three prophets to lay their hands upon me to pray for my wife and I as leaders of the church. While praying they began to prophesy to me that God was calling me to leave the local church and be a Prophet to the Nations. This was a dramatic event and yet the elders of the church also bore witness to the direction that came.

In a similar way to the church in Antioch, my own leaders prayed and released me to the task. At that time I had not travelled outside of Canada apart from some trips to the USA and UK.

God did not tell Paul and his team where they were going or how they would be supported or how long they would be gone, but the leadership team simply stood in faith with them. I also had no idea where God would direct me but in the years that followed I visited many nations and ministered in many streams, and always with the conviction that when God speaks we must give immediate and careful obedience to what He asks of us. The result of this has been the blessing of God on the church and the continual supply of personal provision for Nova and I.

There is a much greater place for the Spirit of prophecy to influence the leaders of our churches. The foundation of the word is important but we must not strategize on the grounds of intellect and principle alone. A prophetic church will want the Spirit and the Word to agree together in their decisions and in their mode of operations.

Sharing prophetic resources

After we had been there a number of days, a prophet named Agabus came down from Judea. (Acts 21: 10)

Although we don't see it illustrated in the Acts narrative in the context of their own meetings, the Jerusalem church had obviously developed in prophetic ministry. Along with Agabus, the Antioch church received encouragement from the prophets Judas and Silas before they returned to those who had sent them.[17]

It is interesting to note that Agabus travelled in a team with other credible men. He was not a 'loose cannon' or a 'floating kidney in the body of Christ', but a man sent from Jerusalem under authority and for this precise reason could be received by the church in Antioch. Later on we see him joining in the work at Ceasarea in Acts 21.

Unlike the present-day USA, no prophetic church centres existed in the New Testament. Rather, prophets were released from their local church to assist others. Alarm bells ring even more loudly when I hear comments such as "All the Prophets are moving here", and "We need to re-establish OT styles of worship like they had in the Temple". Such statements challenge authentic New Testament church life community and practice and usually originate from mystics who no longer see the need for personal and corporate evangelism.

[17] Acts 15: 30-33

Some Prophets choose to separate themselves from the local church entirely and to operate in independence as though nothing on earth was good enough for them. Such independence has proved responsible for acrimonious relationships between leaders of local churches and external prophetic ministries. In my early years of prophetic ministry, I certainly found myself sometimes in tense situations with local churches. In one church where spiritual gifts were somewhat rare I had a strong prophetic word and wanted to bring it to a crowded meeting. At the first moment of quiet I began to speak but immediately those in authority moved to prevent me. Unfortunately for them, my young companions were quite 'anti-establishment' and quickly formed a wall between us. So unhindered I delivered my word, which was a good one but totally out of order. On the other hand, there was a failure of those leading the meeting to allow space for the moving of the Spirit.

God never envisaged prophets and local churches as separate entities but as one unit achieving his purposes in the earth. Undoubtedly this requires wisdom and understanding on both sides and as my experience shows, sometimes both can get it wrong at the same time!

Working out prophetic ministry

There is a need in local churches for several types of ministry:

- Local prophetic teams made up of those who have prophetic gifting in the local church and whom the church will allow to operate freely within.

- Travelling acknowledged prophets who are able to train local church prophetic teams, and bring specific direction to the leaders of local churches regarding their mission and strategy for growth and extension.

- Travelling acknowledged prophets who can bring prophecies to local church members to help them know their place of mission and ministry and give them prophetic words by which they can fight the good fight of faith.

In the many years spent with the three churches in Taiwan we have felt led by God to build a pattern of prophetic operation that could be reproduced throughout the country. These churches are now amongst the fastest growing in their nation with congregations now in the thousands.

One of these, Banner Church in Taichung, was less than fifty people but over a twelve year period has grown to more than two thousand. I attribute such dramatic growth to them taking very seriously the prophetic direction we have given during this time. Welcoming regular visits and input from prophets their trust has proven to be very effective. They have also seriously set about raising up and releasing their own prophetic team in the local church. As a result, prophetic ministry from Banner Church is now going out into the nation and they have become a church that replicates New Testament activities in many ways.

This is only one example of many I could show you to emphasise that prophetic ministry is more than a theory or idealistic projection: it works in real life as those inside and outside the local church are harnessed together in biblical partnership. Prophets can play their part in achieving this by:

● Understanding they are not building their own kingdoms

I will build my church, and the gates of Hades will not overcome it. (Matthew 16: 18)

The great apostle, Jesus, is committed to building no other organization than his Church. He has no alternative plan or second choice. Ephesians 3: 10 reveals the intention of Jesus that through the Church the wisdom of God should be revealed to 'the rulers and authorities in the heavenly realms'.

● Experiencing the benefits of co-operation

Indeed working with local churches releases them to their highest potential. The picture of the lonely prophet which we often have projected is out of step with the New Testament Church pattern. Working in teams as happened in Antioch, their worth was unquestionable and must have brought great comfort to them in the difficult times they lived. Furthermore, being 'sent' as they were in the case of those from Jerusalem would have also been a source of strength. For these men did not come out of their own choosing but out of a truly submitted relationship to their own local church in Jerusalem. Their potential was thus increased because they did not see themselves as individuals but as part of a team of builders, willingly co-operating with others in the plan of God to build his church.

● Valuing the voices of other prophets

Rather than seeing themselves as the exclusive voice of God, locally or trans-locally, prophets can learn from and enjoy operating with others. In the formative years of my prophetic ministry I had many experiences of team-working which came as we ministered into local churches on an annual basis. These were always great times of learning albeit not always in a positive way!

On one such occasion I worked alongside a man who always wanted to be the first to prophesy over our candidates. He would rush out of his seat and make sure he was the initial 'voice'. As one of the other two prophets, I noticed that when we returned to our seats after prophesying he would always say: "You know, the Lord showed me exactly the same stuff as you guys bought but I just didn't say it".

He had a problem! He always wanted to be able to demonstrate his gift as superior to ours both privately and in public. He failed to understand that God has no 'stars' and indeed any prophetic person should keep in mind that in Numbers 22 God spoke through a donkey! The Scripture tells us that God is no respecter of persons and affirms us all as members of one body. What is most important about any of us is simply belonging to him.

On the other hand, local church leaders must see the prophetic ministry as an asset not a threat to the flock. The visit of Judas and Silas to Antioch was warmly received and resulted in a deposit of ministry into the body that would be a part of its foundation. Their goal was to encourage and strengthen and this has not changed to day with those who are credible prophetic ministries.

After spending some time there, they were sent off by the brothers with the blessing of peace to return to those who had sent them. (Acts 15: 33)

There was no question of fear on the part of the leaders. They welcomed the two prophets among them, and sent them on their way with blessing. It was the same with Agabus and his team when they visited on another occasion. The confidence of the church leaders in both cities was well founded when the predicted famine came to pass.

Prophets without local churches to work out their ministry are disconnected from their true function. In the same way churches without regular, credible prophetic input are missing a whole dimension in their energy, strategy and vision. A great need in all churches today is for the demonstration of the supernatural as part of church life, and one of the keys to this is found in the prophetic ministry. If we can enable and allow the church and prophetic ministry to pull together with the same goals, we will then function closely to the New Testament Church pattern.

7 Home-grown and visiting prophets

Memories flood my mind from childhood days when people start to talk about certain things. One of those things is vegetable gardening! During the Second World War, food was in short supply in the UK due to the bombing and German blockades of the sea-lanes. As a result the government encouraged all households to grow their own vegetables and gave them incentives to do so. My dad, like most other men in our village, had a big vegetable garden at the rear of our home and also rented a piece of ground across the street for growing even more vegetables. So we, along with most of our neighbours, were self-sufficient in this area.

Sunday mornings were often spent out in the yard with my dad picking up potatoes and later sitting on the doorstep to shell the peas. We soon all agreed that home-grown crops were simply the best! After all, as long as we planted at the right time, not only could we be assured of their availability but also we could influence their growth by nurturing them well. Furthermore, the vegetables that reached us from other locations, simply tasted worse according to the time spent in transit.

Today, we are hearing many of the same arguments as economies struggle and some households find it more advantageous to return to the old ways of relative self-sufficiency. Home-grown is becoming increasingly popular in towns and cities across the world as people rediscover what their fathers and grandfathers knew well about food production.

What has this to do with the prophetic ministry? Firstly, as we have already established, there is a great need for the encouragement and blessing of the prophetic ministry in the local church. Like vegetables it is one of the staple foods of the church and we need to be assured of its availability and not leave this precious gift subject to the plans of others. Secondly, home-production of the prophetic ministry means that what arises can be better than that which has travelled a long way and which may not be totally 'the flavour' we appreciate! Also, the opportunity to grow and nurture the prophetic ministry in the local church means the leaders there can play a part in nurturing and growing it from scratch.

Home-grown

Since, the early 1990s I have been pleased to see a hunger for the 'home-grown' in prophetic ministry in the local church. When I first stepped out into this area, it involved lots of long journeys. Churches from all over North America would call and ask for my participation in travelling prophetic teams that were invited to visit them for 5 or 6 days at a time to minister to their flock.

These gatherings were called Presbytery Meetings: a reference to Paul's letter to Timothy in reference to the time that hands had been laid on him and prophecies had been made over him. There was a shortage of prophetic ministries in those days available to local assemblies who wanted prophetic input for their members. But the cost of bringing this kind of ministry to a small church was very high as it involved paying their fares and giving them a reasonable honorarium.

So in the early 1990s some of us began to plan to raise up other prophets who would be available in their own vicinity and also to train up teams in the larger local churches who could go into their own house churches, cell groups and discipleship groups to minister specifically to people as the Presbytery teams had previously done. This took some time since prophets unlike cabbages are not quickly and easily grown.

This strategy began in North America and our particular team extended the teaching and training to other countries including the UK and Taiwan where there was great need for such ministry and much hunger.

Even today most strong prophetic ministries are more than a little tired from the calls they have on their time and gift and many are at a place of near exhaustion. Burn-out among such ministries is not unusual and casualties abound from over-exposure of young and immature ministries to extended exhaustive ministry. But now, we are able to point to places in Canada, USA, Europe and Taiwan especially, where local churches have raised up their own prophetic teams. They minister in their own church and out into the surrounding areas to others with great success.

Just as in the churches of Jerusalem and Antioch, I believe that God is restoring this kind of prophetic community within local churches today. However, a mindset still exists to discredit and to deny the present operation of the gifts of the Spirit, of which Prophecy is one. But the failures of the past and the destruction that has dogged the prophetic ministry must not be allowed to cause its shutdown at a time when its influence is so desperately needed in our local churches and the world. Similarly, I have been in churches that welcomed me as a visiting Prophet, but were in terror of any of their own people ever beginning to operate in a similar fashion, in case of some ghastly aberration occurring that they would not know how to deal with.

The context of worship

How can we see a prophetic team becoming a vital part of the local church and adding a dimension to the lives of all who belong to it? Most importantly, a prophetic atmosphere or soil is needed in which to develop. Samuel was able to understand this and when he met Saul who was to be king of Israel he gave him instructions that would unlock the gift of prophecy in him which to this point was hidden.

After that you will go to Gibeah of God, where there is a Philistine outpost. As you approach the town, you will meet a procession of prophets coming down from the high place with lyres, tambourines, flutes and harps being played before them, and they will be prophesying. The Spirit of the LORD will come upon you in power, and you will prophesy with them; and you will be changed into a different person. (1 Samuel 10: 5-6)

It is helpful to realize that Saul had never prophesied to this point. He was simply regarded as a 'donkey boy' employed by his father to ensure their herd was protected and fed. A prophet will see the potential in people in their various roles in the church regardless of how they appear to everyone else.

Also notable is the context of worship for the prophetic ministry to come forth. Within the dynamic activity of focusing upon God and acknowledging his wonders, the Holy Spirit moves in power. Elsewhere in 2 Kings 3: 14-16, the seasoned prophet Elisha recognizes the need for such an atmosphere when approached for his service by three allied Kings at the onset of war against Moab. "Bring me a harpist" he requested and while the harpist played the Spirit of the Lord inspired him to give the desired prophetic word.

Such supernatural activity continued during times of prayer and praise into and throughout the New Testament. In Antioch they worshipped and fasted in expectancy. During one such time Paul and Barnabas were singled out for the work they were called to do. Therefore a church that is wanting to grow prophetically should have a similar dynamic activity of worship in its meetings. It is quite appropriate to suppose that where praise and worship freely flow, people are more like to be released into spiritual gifts. Worship leaders have a positive part to play in such times and need to be more than just good musicians. They may be the source of a liberating move of the Holy Spirit as they seek to be sensitive to his activity. Not only will prophets flourish in this environment but also those with other giftings. In the case of Saul it released him to be a mouthpiece for God.

Order

Despite what some may think, the prophetic atmosphere should not be one of total openness as this would (and often does) lead to much harm being caused. People grow best in an atmosphere where they are aware of boundaries and their words being subject to the consideration of others. It is not uncommon to hear words that are merely outbursts of criticism. In 1 Corinthians 14 19: 23, Paul says only two or three prophets should speak and that what they say should be weighed carefully. He also calls for order and for sensitivity in allowing others to input. Prophets are not compelled to 'give their word' the moment it is received but rather when appropriate.

The key here is lack of dominance by either prophetic people or leaders. In a right atmosphere 'weighing' of the validity of prophetic words will be done with grace on the part of the leadership and with submission on the part of the person bringing the word. Rancour on either side leads to tension and a lack of freedom to participate and constitutes a 'putting out of the Spirits fire'. This will of course hinder any attempt to build a growing prophetic constituency in the local church.

Dampening worship by too much control will ultimately dampen prophetic release. Conservative forms of leadership are often more concerned with the small details of managing the meeting than with allowing the Holy Spirit freedom to move. People who are sensitive to the Holy Spirit are also conscious of the attitude that continually ties the exercise of corporate worship to a timetable that makes no place for any moving in the realms of revelation. Rambling through a long morning of worship without direction is not a welcome experience, but on the other hand a 'safe' policy that cuts off the moving of the Spirit will eventually lead to sterility.

Welcoming environment

When prophets and prophetic people are given freedom to move in the local church there will come a revelation and direction concerning those who are also prophetic.

So Elijah went from there and found Elisha son of Shaphat. He was plowing with twelve yoke of oxen, and he himself was driving the twelfth pair. Elijah went up to him and threw his cloak around him. (1 Kings 19: 19-20)

Just as Elijah was able to respond to God and make a call to prophetic ministry to Elisha, so also prophets today will identify others with similar calling and place their mantle or stamp of approval and recognition on the individual. This has sometimes been my privilege while ministering. As an indication of what I am sensing, I sometimes take my jacket and throw it over them as a sign. I will also confer with the leaders of their church and point out what I consider to be an exceptional gift within that person.

A church that embraces prophetic ministry and regular input from prophets will also attract believers with similar calling or interest who perhaps have no encouragement or outlet in their own environment. Thus in these two ways a prophetic pool or seedbed will develop in the congregation and a team created. This is not neither a Charismatic program or the latest 'bandwagon' to jump on in order to be known as 'cutting edge'. Prophetic teams do not just happen and it is foolish to regard them as a great idea and suddenly look to create one internally or say "Let's hire this person from here and encourage that other person to join our church so we can put it together in a couple of months." Prophetic teams are organic and grow and develop locally out of a genuine desire to see the church develop a balanced lifestyle that includes biblical soundness and Holy Spirit reality.

Developing a team

Those who have been identified as having a developing prophetic gift in the church need to be gathered together perhaps at monthly intervals initially. Making a 'grand announcement' to the congregation is not particularly advisable as it may put unnecessary pressure to perform on the people selected.

An elder or responsible member of the leadership team is best suited to lead these meetings. Prayer and seeking God together for the church should be high on the agenda along with teaching from the leader on the place of prophecy and its various manifestations. As the group develops, confidence and wisdom for participating individually in corporate meetings will be gained. They will also understand the framework for operating in freedom but under the constraint of knowing their contribution will be evaluated by the leaders.

Through praying together, some, revelation, visions and prophetic insight related to the church will undoubtedly occur. This information can be judged within the team and the Leader can refer back to the wider leadership team anything that seems worthy of pursuing. As the group grows in maturity, all the leaders from time to time will want to join with them and seek some supernatural insight into the direction and ministry of the church.

I remember one occasion when a local church was considering taking on a new staff member and had asked the church membership to submit any thoughts they had concerning the suitability of this person into full-time leadership. A prophetic team was already established in the church and they prayed into the possibility of this new team member joining the staff. But as they prayed it became increasingly apparent that God was showing them it to be an inappropriate choice. Their misgivings were conveyed to the leadership in most humble and non-judgmental terms but the leaders chose to reject the advice and go ahead. After a few months their error became clear and the person was released from the role with some difficulty. Accordingly the leadership apologized to the prophetic team and from this time on recognized the importance of their insight. A good relationship was formed as confidence developed on both sides.

Local church prophetic teams will also be greatly helped by the input of visiting prophets and as such, time should be set apart for them to spend together. Their meetings may include teaching from the prophet, the releasing of greater anointing and also of question and answer style interaction. There is good precedent for this in the Scripture:

Elijah took his cloak, rolled it up and struck the water with it. The water divided to the right and to the left, and the two of them crossed over on dry ground. When they had crossed, Elijah said to Elisha, "Tell me, what can I do for you before I am taken from you?" "Let me inherit a double portion of your spirit," Elisha replied. "You have asked a difficult thing," Elijah said, "yet if you see me when I am taken from you, it will be yours – otherwise not." (2 Kings 2: 8-10)

Earlier on we saw that Samuel gave an instruction to Saul that he must fulfil certain conditions and when he did so he was released in the prophetic gift. So also here Elisha is expected to pursue God and stick with Elijah to obtain an increased anointing. It is critical for members of local church prophetic teams that they pursue increasing anointing and revelation especially when they can be exposed to prophets and strong prophetic ministries who pass through the church.

There is much to be said on the subject of local church prophetic teams, and there are doubtless more insights to be shared as examples of this ministry become clear in church life. Again we need to be reminded that such teams are organic and will not always look the same in their final form.

'Visiting' prophets

*Now Moses said to Hobab son of Reuel the Midianite, Moses'
father-in-law, "We are setting out for the place about which the
LORD said, 'I will give it to you.' Come with us and we will treat
you well, for the LORD has promised good things to Israel." He
answered, "No, I will not go; I am going back to my own land and
my own people." But Moses said, "Please do not leave us. You
know where we should camp in the desert, and you can be our
eyes. If you come with us, we will share with you whatever good
things the LORD gives us."* (Numbers 10: 29-32)

This is an interesting story here of need and supply. It is not
hard to see that Hobab is a picture of the Prophet while Moses
is in the role of an Apostle. Moses recognised that this man
was the 'eyes' of Israel, a very obvious picture of a prophet,
and that the journey would be safer and much enhanced if he
accompanied them.

In a similar way, local churches need a prophetic voice and
direction to protect them and to bring them to their destiny.
It is quite obvious that the church in Antioch had a strong
relationship externally with Agabus as well as a strong
relationship internally with their own prophetic team. He was
a frequent visitor whose prophetic direction was well received
by the church leaders. He does not appear to have dominated
them in any way. He simply added a dimension that was not
present amongst the prophets and elders in the local church.

Over the years I have had the privilege of fulfilling such a
role to churches in North America, and internationally. Some
of them were asking me based on principles alone, others
out of sincere relationship. For Moses and Hobab this was
a relationship which carried with it responsibility as well as
benefit. However, it sprung from relationship not principle. In
the natural sense they were son and father-in-law and out of
this there came a spiritual dimension.

My own experience has been that when local churches are willing to invite prophetic ministry to specifically relate to them in a long term role, there is a short and long term benefit for both parties. One church where I was involved in this role, invited me in every year for more than ten years, but to my knowledge never once did the leadership apply the prophetic to the church or the individuals in their congregation. This was not only a sad thing from my perspective but even more that the church and individuals failed to grow to their potential in God. This relationship was one that flowed from the principle that churches need prophetic input on a regular basis. On the other hand I have had gloriously successful long term relationships with churches and individuals that have grown exponentially and where individuals found and walked out their destinies. These were based on real relationship not just with the leaders but with the whole fellowship.

Moses invitation included providing for Hobab as he journeyed with them and a church should do likewise. Practically speaking this means becoming part of the prophet's financial support system in response to his commitment to walk with them through strategy and vision in the days ahead.

Prior to the journey

Before beginning such a journey together, a few things need to be established between the two parties. Prophets need first to understand that they are engaged on a long-term mission with the churches they serve. It is essential that they build relationship with the church leaders and credibility with the congregation. Patience and a real commitment to grow with each church is required rather than flitting between them like bees from one flower to another. Sadly, the need of financial support has often been a greater motivator to some prophetic ministries than the direct leading of the Holy Spirit in deciding their personal itinerary.

For many years I simply itinerated through churches that invited me. In this process, I was sometimes exploited by people for their own purposes. I was drastically underpaid, but still built some lasting relationships. God spoke to me clearly and said that I would be better to focus on a few churches where I could make maximum input and gain long term results. When I began to deliberately do this I was and still am amazed at the outcome. Today I see churches around the world that have blossomed and grown out of the established relationship we have had together.

Working with leaders of individual local churches and speaking into their own personal lives as well as the life of the congregation cannot be quickly achieved – credibility takes time. Of course every coin has two sides and on the other is the expectation and attitude of the local church and its leaders toward prophetic ministry. There must be an invitation into the life of the local church. Moses said to his father-in-law, "Come with us and we will do you good". Neither took the relationship for granted because of their family connection. But Hobab did have the opportunity to opt out and was not bound simply by their natural association.

Churches looking for long term prophetic input should consider the following as basic requirements:

- The standard of the Bible is held higher than any denominational views or traditional values related to religious culture. As such, they should be willing and able to conform their activities and government accordingly.

- A willingness to receive prophets in their biblical role and not as Christian fortune tellers. The gifting is to be used strategically in the church rather than as entertainment for the congregation.

- A real commitment to build a relationship of trust and honesty with the prophetic ministry and not simply an official one.

- The promotion of a prophetic atmosphere where individuals are free to operate whether the 'visiting' prophet is present or absent. This also includes stewarding and acting upon prophetic words that come to the church
- Just as with Hobab and Moses there should be a commitment to 'do the prophet good' in return for his long term commitment to the church. This means undertaking to be part of the financial support network of the prophet.

Without any of these undertakings, prophetic input will not have its full effect and may even be counter-productive. For instance, apathy will arise when prophetic direction cannot be instituted because of vestiges of denominational structure. I have prophesied in churches where the five ministry gifts and eldership were not recognized as valid for today. Thus when I point out people called to be elders, nothing happens because of the non-biblical structure. If the structure cannot be changed the prophetic word 'falls by the wayside'.

When there is no receptivity to the strategy given the prophetic ministry is devalued in the eyes of the congregation. Churches that continue to try and blend programmed Christianity with prophetic direction frequently waste time and finances.

Timothy, my son, here are my instructions for you, based on the prophetic words spoken about you earlier. May they give you the confidence to fight well in the Lord's battles. Cling tightly to your faith in Christ, and always keep your conscience clear. For some people have deliberately violated their consciences; as a result, their faith has been shipwrecked. (1 Timothy 1: 18-19 NLT)

Paul tells Timothy how important the prophetic words he received are to the warfare he is engaged in. This is why it is vital to follow through on prophetic words as a strategy in the local church. If there is no commitment to do this then Prophets are actually wasting their time and gifting and 'sowing their seed' on stony ground that will yield no fruit.

My conversations with other prophets confirms that the greatest frustration is how rarely their words are applied by local church leaders. Instead their words are frequently rated against other prophetic words and like ornaments left to gather dust on shelves.

8 Great expectations

Immediately after finishing High School at 16 years of age, I found employment as a file clerk in one of the record offices of the local County Council. My new boss was a man who had succeeded well in the department and we quickly developed a rapport. The work involved much interdepartmental activity locating and transferring files. My boss was well pleased with me and had great confidence in my ability to find lost items. Accordingly when others mislaid or lost files or papers he would announce boldly "My boy will find them and bring them to your office". Initially the encouragement was quite motivating but as time went on I realized that people now relied on me in this role, and had developed 'great expectations'. By the grace of God (I was a brand new Christian at the time) I never failed to produce, but there were pressures associated with this.

In a similar way, people with prophetic ministries are subjected to 'great expectations' by both individuals and churches as corporate bodies. This naturally creates an awesome sense of dependence on God as any words uttered will potentially influence the destiny of recipients and perhaps even that of nations! Being prophetic is exciting and motivational but it is important to recognise and even be wary of the pressures which result from this amazing gift that God gives.

"Teacher we want to see a miraculous sign from you" (Matt 12: 38)

Jesus was constantly pressured by those around him for a demonstration of the miraculous. In his early ministry he rejected the pressure by saying "my time has not yet come". John the Baptist enquired of him whether he was the predicted Anointed One or should the people be looking for someone else. There was pressure in this question because

John was looking for supernatural confirmation of Jesus ministry on an ongoing basis. Sometimes when in a corporate situation or even talking to an individual I can sense what is going on in their spirit. They are saying to themselves as I share or preach, "Why doesn't he hurry up and get on with prophesying; this is what I really want to hear!" The pressure here is subtle but occasionally it can be blatant and make prophets feel they simply have to submit.

Balaam found himself in a similar position in the Old Testament[18] after his gifting became known to Balak, the King of Moab. Israel had left Egypt and destroyed the armies of the nations that opposed them on their journey. Now they were encamped next to Moab and the king was rightly worried about his future prospects. So he sent princely messengers to Baalam, offering payment in return for a curse on these unwelcome neighbours. But God told him not to curse those whom were in fact blessed.

When Balak learnt that the prophet had refused to return with his messengers, he sent even more distinguished princes in greater number. Accompanying the intended flattery was a great reward and an open invitation to ask anything of the king. Once again Balaam resisted temptation and turned to the Lord for guidance. This time he was told to go with them but only to do what the Lord told him. On arrival, Balak released his irritation with a barrage of questions concerning why Balaam had not responded at once. In short, he threw a tantrum!

A comparable display of immaturity is portrayed in Luke 7: 31-32 concerning the people of Israel. Jesus describes them as children expecting others to dance simply because they played the flute and to cry when they sang a lament. He flatly refused to meet any expectations that did not match with those that came from God. Balaam was the same and told Balak, "I must speak only what God puts in my mouth."

[18] Numbers 22: 14-38

Balaam was a man with a proven prophetic ministry and could have used this situation to advance his own reputation. He could have also found himself financially more secure if he responded to this situation. There was an expectation placed on him that was an attractive one and could have additionally fed his own vanity.

Expectations come in many forms

Pressure to perform arises in a variety of ways, one of which is what I call the 'just one more request'. In the process of a meeting I and others with me have the opportunity to minister to many people. Sometimes a long flight plus a demanding schedule leaves us exhausted at the end of the evening. A well-meaning local leader, trying to get the most for his congregation, will approach with something along the lines of, "I know you are tired, but we have just one more. This person is at a real crossroads and needs a clear word right now".

Such a scenario can lead to disaster since the prophet is no longer focused and the clear flow of the Holy Spirit is clouded or perhaps finished. Neither the prophet, who is sincerely attempting to serve, and the candidate who may desperately be seeking a way forward are helped. "Will you please bring me a word from the Lord?" also seems like a reasonable request. However, prophets and prophetic people are not like fortune-tellers to be 'consulted'. This concept comes from the Old Covenant and is nowhere modelled in the book of Acts nor the Epistles.

In ancient times entering into the presence of the King was literally an awesome thing. Coming to him meant that you knew your place and waited expectantly. The initiative in speaking was always with the King. The subject never initiated the conversation. So it is in the prophetic realm that God ought to be the initiator. The Prophet is listening but not obliged to say anything that God does not himself instigate.

"I believe the Lord revealed that you have a prophetic word for me" is another forthright attempt to pressure someone into giving a prophetic utterance that they have not actually received from the Lord. Spiritual control is also being sought with the implied suggestion of having an equal anointing at least to that of the prophet. He must therefore dig deeply into his gifting in order to produce a word for them.

More than once I have been approached with the loaded request, "I have a gift for you but would you pray for me first? I only want prayer you don't have to prophesy". When asked what to pray, the answer comes: "Just whatever the Lord shows you." The feeling here is of being bribed into bringing a word or giving some particular direction. Frequently these people are in a situation where others are receiving and time is growing short or the meeting has finished. Dissatisfied with the perceived 'extra blessings' being heaped on their brothers and sisters in Christ they use this tactic to 'jump ahead in the queue'.

Often in oriental situations, another pressure comes into play. "Brother, a very important (and usually rich) person has just come into the meeting. You should give him a word, because he is very influential. Maybe God will show the prophet something to share with him!" Submitting to this expectation is potentially dangerous and definitely unscriptural. It could also be embarrassing and unfair on the person and the church, since popularity and riches do not influence God in whom he chooses to speak to.

Standing firm

Jesus often faced these problems but strongly resisted the pressure placed upon him by those around, no matter how important or influential they were. In Matthew 12: 39 the people wanted a miraculous sign to prove his identity but none was offered other than a reference to the sign of Jonah. Before handing Jesus over to the Romans, the ruling

Jews mocked him with the words "Prophesy to us. Christ. Who hit you?"[19]

Not all requests or provocations met with a flat refusal. When asked by the disciples to reveal the time of his return, he responded that:

"No one knows about that day or hour, not even the angels in heaven, nor the Son, but only the Father." (Matthew 24: 36)

While this reply was specifically aimed at their question, Jesus also emphasized that God will not tell us all we want to know at the time we want to know it. God is the initiator in revelation and discloses secrets as he chooses. On another occasion, Jesus said that he only said the things he heard his Father saying. As our prophetic model, we should follow his example.

Jesus gave them this answer: *"I tell you the truth, the Son can do nothing by himself; he can do only what he sees his Father doing, because whatever the Father does the Son also does. For the Father loves the Son and shows him all he does. Yes, to your amazement he will show him even greater things than these.* (John 5: 19-20)

In 1 Corinthians 11: 23, the apostle Paul wrote that he was passing on what had been received from the Lord. In all these instances of Scripture we see that the jurisdiction should be of God and not of any human agency. We therefore need to be careful to understand that prophecy must not be confused in anyway with fortune telling. Balaam had to make it clear that he was not going to prophesy either for money or for the satisfaction of others. He did not see himself as a prophetic machine.

The advent of the new covenant gives us all direct access to God. The Scriptures say: *If any of you lacks wisdom, he should ask God, who gives generously to all without finding fault, and it will be given to him.* (James 1: 5)

[19] Matthew 26: 68

Much prophecy is about bringing confirming words to the people being ministered to. Intimidating expectations such as those mentioned above need to be avoided if possible or resisted. They test the integrity and challenge the humility of prophetic people. Sometimes it may seem easier to bring a word from our own spirit rather than simply tell them you have nothing to say. When training prophetic ministries I tell them to accept that we do not have a word for everything that is happening personally and corporately. Thinking otherwise, particularly as a result of pressure from others, serves simply to cheapen or prostitute this precious gift of God.

Right expectations

Sometimes I have been asked by leaders of churches, "What can we expect of you while you are here?" There are right expectations for those who are called to be a part of prophetic ministry, whether locally or trans-locally.

Prophetic people should not want to have special treatment from the local church. In Ephesians 4: 25, we see that we are all members of one body. Every believer has an equal relationship with God. All gifting is from God and no one should be regarded as 'extra-special' because of receiving a prophetic blessing. In addition, prophetic people should come under the authority of the local leaders who participate in the judging (weighing) of the words which are given. The prophetic ministry should humbly and willing submit to this and be glad for the safety it brings. If the leadership has requests then the prophetic people should be careful to honour them. For example, a candidate may be put forth but the leadership request that if the prophets sense a leadership call, they not mention it publicly but discuss it with the leaders privately. Paul said to Timothy:

But you, keep your head in all situations, endure hardship, do the work of an evangelist, discharge all the duties of your ministry. (2 Timothy 4: 5)

As prophets serve they must face up to not being some kind of specialist meriting higher status than fellow believers. I have counted it great joy in my working with leaders of the underground church in China, to go through the same life experience as they regularly do as believers in China. Once I found myself detained and questioned by the Chinese police and subjected to some intense pressure. What a joy! On another occasion I lay hidden in the bushes on a mountainside, while the secret police searched the whole area to find us. This was not a time to say to God, "Why me?" but rather to rejoice that we had been found worthy to undergo such an experience.

Prophetic people should not consider themselves to be anything approaching 'prima donnas', sometimes unwilling to serve because of the lack of ideal conditions or even the state of their mood on a particular day. Peter writes that every member of the body of Christ should use the gifts they have received to, "serve others, faithfully administering God's grace in its various forms".[20]

If they are gifted and God has indeed given a word, the church should be able to rely on them to bring that word of encouragement or direction no matter the personal season they find themselves in. The gift is not given as a personal treasure to horde but rather to bring whenever appropriate in the service of the church. Part of this expectation involves actively stirring up the gift as opportunity presents itself, and not simply sitting on the sidelines. Paul told Timothy:

For this reason I remind you to fan into flame the gift of God, which is in you through the laying on of my hands. (2 Timothy 1: 6)

The onus is constantly on those in positions of responsibility to 'fan their gift into flame'. It is not to be left to the worship leader or of others leading prayer and intercession, although of course the help they do give is of great value. Fervent

[20] 1 Peter 4: 10

personal prayer and worship is required rather than allowing oneself to become sloppy and detached from God. Determination is needed to avoid becoming sluggish in using spiritual gifts and always the treasures of mercy and grace remain available to help on the journey.

Being sensitive and accountable

I have already mentioned briefly how once when taking prophetic meetings with others of similar gifting, I became increasingly bemused by one of our number who felt it necessary to take centre-stage by being the first to prophesy. Every meeting, at the first available sniff of air space, his voice rang out and proceeded on a 'long-haul' flight of domination.

Prophetic people need to be sensitive not only to God but also to each other, ensuring that those in team with them are given equal opportunity to share any inspiration. Seeking to bring order to the Corinthian church, Paul acknowledges that more than one person will be operating in the same spiritual gift and calls for sensitivity and respect.[21] "For those who are prophets, only two or three should speak, and on the understanding that what they say will be weighed carefully." I have sadly experienced men and women who regarded themselves as exempt from this requirement due to their fame. Similarly those intent on their own agenda are horrified at the thought they might be questioned on the veracity of their words. No matter how popular or mature a prophet may consider himself, he should always expect to have his prophetic words evaluated by other team members and those in authority. This also acts as an important test of the humility and servant heart of such a person.

Being prophetic does not give anyone license to maul the body of Christ and treat it with contempt by being unaccountable. Travelling around the world I see and hear

[21] 1 Corinthians 14: 26-33

of instances where people are challenged concerning the value of their prophetic words and their response is simply, "I am a prophet, what I speak is from God". Perhaps they are modelling themselves somewhat on Old Testament prophets who were scathing about those who questioned their word. Their lives depended on accuracy, especially as mechanisms for judging or weighing a word were not established until New Testament times. Problems obviously arise when someone wants to be a combination of both Old and New Testament prophet. Ignorant claims to infallibility have done much damage to the cause of present-day prophetic movement and brought chaos and confusion to many a church.

The Prophets we see in the book of Acts moved in a new design under a New Covenant. They did not attempt to mix in or blend in Old Covenant prophetic concepts. Rather, they realized that what had gone before was passing away:

By calling this covenant 'new' he has made the first one obsolete: and what is obsolete and aging will soon disappear.
(Hebrews 8: 13)

For some 'prophets' this passing has proved difficult to grasp as they attempt to remain in a place of no accountability. Even worse, just as in the movie 'Grumpy Old Men', some seem to have a mission to make the rest of the church feel bad. Proudly they build their character and personality around the myth that prophets simply have to be disagreeable characters due to their calling. Hence the popular explanation for bizarre and anti-social Christians is "Ah, it's because they're prophetic!

Being a Prophet should not mean not being like a reincarnated John the Baptist but rather like Jesus: a lover of men and women and a friend of children. Neither should it mean purposefully acting as a lone-ranger, aloof and uninvolved with other members of the body of Christ as they attempt to fulfil their God-given callings. Prophets are simply those with a mission and a calling that allows them to speak the heart of God to individuals and local churches as equal members of the same body. They are called to manifest grace and love in their dealings with the Church. As the scripture says: *Let your conversation be always full of grace, seasoned with salt, so that you may know how to answer everyone.* (Colossians 4: 6)

9 Pits and cisterns

Once I was approached by a woman who said, "God has shown me that you have a prophetic word for me". What a pressure this was, especially since I had no notion of any such revelation at all. In effect she was claiming a stronger anointing than I, since God had only spoken to her. Under such circumstances, some prophets will feel enticed to offer something harmless to appease the person, yet their words may come back to haunt them in the days ahead. As for me I simply told the lady, "I DO have a word for you ...Go away!" Something in my spirit immediately picked up that this was a trap set by a 'superficially spiritual' person determined to receive a prophetic word by manipulation.

Prophets are especially vulnerable to such approaches at the end of meetings when tired and out of focus. If they succumb then their reputation can be adversely affected. Leaders should be vigilantly protective at these times rather than leaving them exposed to this sort of danger. A prophetic person should only speak what he has seen, heard and been told to say directly from the Holy Spirit.

There is no doubt that the Enemy will do anything to negate the ministry of those who are called to speak as oracles of God. Travelling for many hours and ministering in numerous places leads to intense exhaustion. There are often times of physical and mental fatigue that those not involved in prophetic ministry will not realize.

I heard and my heart pounded, my lips quivered at the sound; decay crept into my bones, and my legs trembled. (Habakkuk 3: 16)

How can I, your servant, talk with you, my lord? My strength is gone and I can hardly breathe. (Daniel 10: 17)

I would personally rather preach for three hours than prophecy for one because of the draining of personal strength. Being exhausted in such a way makes prophetic people vulnerable to the attack of the Enemy, particularly when they are far from home and without the support of family or other team members. Whenever possible, they should travel with someone close as a protection against these things.

Depression and self-pity are constant weapons employed to negate gifting. Like seed from weeds can become planted in tended soil when blown by the wind, thoughts of rejection and being plotted against by supposed enemies spring up and grow unchecked if not dealt with. These can even come after times of great blessing. After a monumental victory over the many prophets of Baal and Asherah, Elijah suddenly became afraid.[22] Not only had he just called down fire from heaven but also ran a considerable distance supernaturally in the power of the Lord. Yet despite the undeniable evidence of God being with him, he ran for his life at the news that Jezebel sought revenge.

While it is true that Elijah did have some grounds for his complaint, he should have been emboldened, perhaps even disdainful of her threats. Yet we find him sitting under a broom tree telling God that he's had enough, that he's a failure and no longer wants to remain alive. Similar unexpected incidents still happen to prophetic people as the Devil does his best to use depression and paranoia about rejection to destroy them. Often the focus of their thoughts are totally unfounded.

Be self-controlled and alert. Your enemy the devil prowls around like a roaring lion looking for someone to devour. Resist him, standing firm in the faith, because you know that your brothers throughout the world are undergoing the same kind of sufferings. (1 Peter 5: 8-9)

[22] 1 Kings 19: 1-10

Prophetic pitfalls

Dangers abound everywhere. Television, the Internet, newspapers and magazines all report from time to time the stories of disgraced Christian ministries now forced to surrender their roles in the community. Sadly a large proportion of these unfortunate people are looked on as prophets, or at least as prophetic in their ministry. It may even be that a powerful anointing has been clearly demonstrated.

The truth is that anyone involved in prophetic ministry can find themselves falling into pits or cisterns that prove to be very destructive and in which they seem to be abandoned by all around them. Often the trap is a careful plan laid by the Enemy to destroy them, their ministry and impact on those around them.

So they took Jeremiah and put him into the cistern of Malkijah, the king's son, which was in the courtyard of the guard. They lowered Jeremiah by ropes into the cistern; it had no water in it, only mud and Jeremiah sank down into the mud. (Jeremiah 38: 6-7)

We find this great prophet of the Old Testament in a very sad state, laying in a pit oozing with mud. He has been snared by his enemies and abandoned by his friends at a time of great need. The reason for imprisonment was because of obediently delivering God's word and not for anything wrong he had done. Like Daniel in the den of lions, Jeremiah was quickly rescued and continued in his ministry. Samson, on the other hand, did not emerge from his time of testing unscathed. A man of similar stature to Jeremiah, he was called to be a national leader and recognized by his enemies as being powerfully able to resist them. His life and ministry became ruined and he ended up totally blind, doing the work of a mule and grinding a mill.

Even the most powerful of prophetic ministries can fall foul to the plans of the enemy which take various forms. The most common snares are as follows:

Money

On one occasion I was invited to teach at a training event in the North of England for budding prophetic ministries. As I prepared for the meetings, the Holy Spirit told me to issue a warning about being led astray by the lure of money. This seemed a rather odd prompting to me, as it would be to anyone familiar with ministry in the UK at that time. Whether prophetic or not, the opportunity for being led astray by being offered too much money was somewhat remote. Despite my misgivings, I still felt convicted to proceed and ventured forth at what seemed the most appropriate time. Perhaps for some, training colleagues of similar profession would be regarded as some sort of pinnacle in their careers. Not by me and certainly not when being faced with howls of somewhat derisive laughter at the irony of my statement.

However, immediately after the event and with the memory of flushed embarrassment still fresh, I left for Taiwan to spend my regular three weeks of intense ministry. On the second night of the meetings, a man came to me and asked "Will you please come to my home and have supper and then prophesy over my family? If you will, I will give you $1000 US as a gift." After this request he then intimated there were other families in the church that would be happy to do the same if not more!! I could have had lunch and supper with two families a day for only 2 hours in each home and came away with $10,000 US! I declined the offer, but was sad to meet a lady the next week doing exactly this for six days a week for three months. She told me quite matter-of-factly, "I do this every year for three months and it finances my worldwide ministry."

This lady was in a pit of her own making. In the previous chapter we read about Balaam having to deal with the pressure of expectation and the lure of financial reward. Both the glamour of recognition from a king and the blessing of material wealth would have appealed to his human nature.

But he stood firm on the ground of wisdom, recognising that succumbing to either would effectively mean a transfer of ownership. "Even if Balak gave me his palace filled with silver and gold, I could not do anything great or small to go beyond the command of the LORD my God." [23]

Balaam saw the danger of allowing money to dictate how and to whom he prophesied. Jesus sternly warned his disciples in Luke 16 that it was impossible to love both God and money. They both demand sovereignty and beckon from opposite poles. It is a curse today that so many in the prophetic world have become entangled in this old enemy, slowly diminishing in their effectiveness and ending up in deserts. With management teams and marketing gurus they arrange events that are little more than fundraisers for personal gain. God is not against his people having money, but is against money having his people. Whether in prophetic ministry or not, problems and pitfalls come from the same source.

Do not love the world or anything in the world. If anyone loves the world, the love of the Father is not in him. For everything in the world – the cravings of sinful man, the lust of his eyes and the boasting of what he has and does – comes not from the Father but from the world. (1 John 2: 15-16)

The craving for things is what causes the strong emphasis on money in many ministries. The desire to live the Hollywood lifestyle is a strong pressure on many to lose their Kingdom perspective and be totally captivated by what they see.

Lust

If the comfort of material wealth seems pleasing to the eye then consider the enticement of sexual attraction. Samson was a miracle baby with a mighty call upon his life, yet the desire of women became his master. Angelic visitations and a word of destiny resulted in a sterile wife giving birth and

[23] Numbers 22: 18

bringing the child up as Nazarite – set apart for God. While visiting Timnor as a young man he saw a beautiful Philistine woman and asked his parents to acquire her as his wife. In the context of his national identity alone, he should not have even considered such a prospect as he was an Israelite called by God not to intermarry with those of other nations. However, once he set his eyes upon her, the lust in his heart took control with disastrous consequences.

The return journey to Timnor with his father and mother did not pass quietly. Suddenly from the wild a young lion sprang upon him with a fearsome roar. But it was the lion and not Samson who perished, such was the strength of the Spirit of the Lord who protected him. For God was using his disobedience as an opportunity to confront the ruling Philistine nation at that time. Nevertheless, Samson did not return home with the focus of his infatuation, for she died violently: burnt to death. The Lord's purposes were accomplished but Samson's only brought him and others heartbreak.

Twenty years later, we find Samson once again on his travels and chasing women. Finally he meets Delilah and the rest of the story is popular history.[24] What perhaps is not so well known is that the source of his strength lay not in locks of hair but rather in God. Ultimately, he allowed lust and desire to grow too powerful and destroy his divine relationship and calling.

Sexual temptation is something that seems to have a particular application to people in prophetic ministry. Revelation and insight into people's lives can sometimes lead to an unhealthy intimacy in relationship with someone of the opposite sex. I could tell many stories of events that I have witnessed and been subjected to in the process of travelling ministry. I have known men to be ambushed by women after a meeting. I have known prophetic ministries who took a different woman to their room each night after the meeting.

[24] Judges 13-16

Some of these women were told what a privilege it was to have sex with 'a great man of God'. I have noticed that when prophets adapt a film-star lifestyle they also begin to believe they live by a different spiritual law. It determines that they are the 'special ones', not subject to the same moral standards as other believers. There are even some who deliberately teach that they are 'manifested sons' and can live by a different code. Behind the scenes there are often others covering their tracks in an attempt to protect their leaders (and sources of income) from exposure to discipline – all of which is very sad.

These situations spring from deceit and from the Enemy, convincing individuals that they are in fact not the same as everyone else in society with regard to moral standard. God requires nothing of them! On the contrary, since prophetic people claim to be messengers of God, they should have higher standards and expectations of themselves. Just like anyone in ministry, prophets are subject to the same temptations as other men. They are not super-beings but, like all of God's children, have supernatural resources available to help.

No temptation has seized you except what is common to man. And God is faithful; he will not let you be tempted beyond what you can bear. But when you are tempted, he will also provide a way out so that you can stand up under it. (1 Corinthians 10: 13)

Pride

Fire keeps us warm, cooks food and burns off paint quite nicely. It also destroys habitats and kills people. Taking pride in oneself is quite healthy when used to look back over past victories as a spur to carry on a good work or to set an example to others. Paul took pride in his conduct in depending on Christ through suffering. He gave the Corinthian church opportunity to take pride in him and his team as an answer to those who took pride in 'what is seen rather than what is in the heart.'[25]

[25] 2 Corinthians 5: 12

Like fire left unchecked, pride can also grow and consume ministries. When words are accurate and popularity grows, it can be easy to start believing the flattering publicity and adding to it. The bandwagon slowly begins rolling. Glossy photographs appear that show no trace of wrinkles and reveal a miraculous set of shiny white teeth. Perhaps the artist even takes time to embellish the smile with an angelic white circle. Seductive slogans such as '100% successful prediction rate!' and 'The Voice to the Nations is coming!' herald tours to major cities. Considering my surname, I quite like 'Those Hazell eyes miss nothing!'

Joking aside, receiving revelation from God is a great privilege, but it has nothing to do with the personal holiness of the individual who prophecies. Pride is a particularly insidious trap for prophets to fall into. If God begins to bestow a ministry with blessing and strong and accurate prophecy, it is quite easy for a person to take the next step and believe that he is infallible. This in turn pressurises people to acclaim him as a great man of God.

If anyone thinks he is something when he is nothing, he deceives himself. Each one should test his own actions. Then he can take pride in himself, without comparing himself to somebody else. (Galatians 6: 3-4)

Pride is often triggered by flattery from those who gather to the ministry. In the beginning they are well-meaning people but ultimately their glowing support ditches the prophet into a pit. Paul spoke of such people in Romans 16: 18. Rather than serving Christ they were merely seeking to satisfy their own appetites and engaged in sweet talk to deceive naive people. Such flattery creates expectation for the prophetic ministry in question to be able to predict any and every event. The person becomes an all-round expert, consulted on the name of the Anti-Christ and the next American president. Eventually he lands up making absurd or totally unbelievable predictions that cause his ministry to be discounted and placed on the lunatic fringe.

Often accompanying such a person's 'expertise' are bizarre actions like kicking people or spitting in their eyes: after all the prophet can now do as he wishes under the 'anointing'. He also become very protective of his 'anointing' and perhaps doesn't want children in the room or anything else that might distract from his being the centre of attention. One prominent prophet placed a paper bag over his head and kept it on between the hotel room and the meeting to avoid 'losing his anointing'. If indeed this could happen, it doesn't say much for the anointing he has in the first place! Another prophet of my acquaintance always came late to the meeting because, "The Lord told me I must eat my evening meal at seven thirty precisely each day". I also know of a prophet being so sure of his revelation that anyone who questioned him about anything was scorned with the words, "Do not lift your hands against the Lords anointed one".

Jealousy

Speakers who are more dynamic than you and students who are brighter. Sportsmen who run quicker, shoot or hit more accurately and who thrive under pressure, whereas you freeze. We're all familiar with the burning sensation of envy that causes our brows to crease and eyes to narrow. Most of the time the feeling is just a gut reaction which we quickly dismiss, perhaps unconsciously or with a shrug and wry smile at ourselves. Not everyone can be the best at everything. With growing maturity we learn to appreciate the skills and qualities in others and perhaps use them as sources of inspiration to improve.

No one sets out to become twisted by jealousy but prophetic people are perhaps more vulnerable than most. Zedekiah was one of a large group of prophets used to telling Ahab the King of Israel exactly what he wanted to hear. Micaiah meanwhile

only spoke what he heard from God and in the words of Ahab
to Jehosophat, King of Judah, "never prophesies anything
good about me, but always bad."[26] The two prophets came
together before the King at a time when he wanted to
know whether to go to war. Along with the other prophets
present, Zedekiah gave encouragement to do so. He had even
carefully made a pair of iron horns to symbolically show Ahab
that he would gore his enemies until they were destroyed.

Micaiah meanwhile had been summoned separately by
name upon the advice of Jehosophat. The messenger who
had heard what the other prophets were saying, advised him
to fall into line and speak favourably. So he did! But it didn't
wash with Ahab. Maybe it was a familiar look of derision on
Micaiah's face that gave the game away or deep sarcasm in
his voice. For Ahab replied, "How many times must I make you
swear to tell me nothing but the truth?"

Like everyone else assembled, Zedekiah heard the King
acknowledge the anointing upon Micaiah and therefore not
upon himself. Further investigation into Ahab reveals a man
who knew that he had incurred God's wrath. It was not for
idle pleasure that an army of prophets were assembled but
because he could no longer count on God's protection. Sure
enough, Micaiah's words were not too pleasing to the ears.
All the prophets proclaiming victory in battle were called liars:
the war would end in disaster and the death of King Ahab.
Unable to contain his indignation, Zedekiah launched forward
in anger and slapped Micaiah in the face.

Outbursts of jealousy are not confined to wicked prophets
but can even happen to sincere ones. This is partly due
to some misunderstandings concerning their ministry.
Sometimes a prophet may feel his gift needs justifying as
being pure and correct to protect his reputation. Jesus neither
felt the need to justify his revelations nor allowed himself to

[26] 1 Kings 22: 8

be influenced by opinions. Rather he took on the very nature of a servant and sought only to be obedient to his Father. Prophets have nothing to protect since they personally are not the source of the message they bring.

Some prophetic people may be insecure in the revelation they have and use jealousy as a protection to bolster their personal confidence. This often arises when they are too hasty and quick to speak before they are sure about what they have heard. Listening carefully is an essential precursor to saying anything on God's behalf. Jealousy also often arises due to comparing personal revelation with that of others and wanting the recognition they receive from those they are ministering too. This can particularly happen to 'old prophets' who feel threatened by the prophetic revelation that comes to younger men and women. God does not favour one above another and all prophets need to make space for God to use any of them without partiality. What they have is a gift from God, not something that has been personally worked for and merited. There are no grounds for jealousy in the prophetic ministry since all are called to recognize and respond to the will of God in choosing whom to speak to and through. Being used by God is not a sign of personal holiness, it is simply by God's grace that they are privileged to speak at all.

10 Wearing the badge

As a young man I lived in England at a time of compulsory military service for all men after their 18th birthday. Not being too keen to enter the army I gave God what I thought was a reasonable choice. He could either provide finance for me to go to Bible school, which would mean temporary exemption from military service, or allow me to serve him within the army. To my surprise, he chose the latter which lasted for two years.

I was not an imposing physical figure, being thin and not very tall. Accordingly, my fellow soldiers paid me little attention until one day when I was given a chevron to sew on my uniform sleeve after being promoted to the rank of Lance Corporal. Amazingly, this badge gave me authority over big muscular men, well above my height and weight. I could, if I wished, instruct them to do unpleasant things and scream expletives of an unpleasant kind in the course of conversation. Fortunately for them, the badge did not change my character and I choose not to abuse the authority given by the Queen to non-commissioned officers. Nevertheless, I did now have considerable authority and accompanying responsibility.

In the charismatic world there is a great thirst for titles, stemming from the belief that a title given, or assumed, reflects a level of spirituality that demands the submission and respect of other Christians. For this reason many in ministry want their names prefixed with 'Pastor' as a sign of their leadership and authority over people. There are also those who thirst for the title 'Prophet' to blow a similar trumpet before their first or surname. However, self-appointment is not something which the body of Christ should encourage or recognize. As my mother would frequently say, "Self praise is no recommendation at all".

Self-appointment

Where I now live in Canada, we have a large Mormon population and it is common to see young men in black suits, carrying the book of Mormon. Those unaware of their purpose may mistakenly regard them as tax collectors or Government officials sweeping the area for illegal workers. Younger folk pinch themselves in disbelief that the villains from last night's film have somehow come to life, while the elderly suspect they may be undertakers on the prowl for business. Frequently these young men come to our door and – being quite short – my first sight is the badge pinned on their chest, proclaiming 'Elder John Doe'. Elder? I am well aware of elders in the Bible and the qualifications for such are quite clearly laid out. These young men, zealous as they are, do not qualify for such a title.

For by the grace given me I say to every one of you: Do not think of yourself more highly than you ought, but rather think of yourself with sober judgment, in accordance with the measure of faith God has given you. (Romans 12: 3)

The people of God need to avoid naming themselves and recognize that, like the young Mormon elders, their designation is meaningless unless they have actually proved able to 'walk in the shoes'. I grew up in a relatively poor family. Although my father worked very hard in the construction industry, his income barely provided for our needs. As such he was no fashion model when it came to dressing. Yet he did have what we called 'Sunday-go-to-meeting' clothes which were for wearing on very special occasions. These clothes were kept in a box as was the custom of most working men of his generation.

Folded neatly in the box were his suit and best shoes kept apart, very black and very shiny. When my parents were absent from the house, I liked to try on the shoes and walk around the bedroom in them. Progress went quite well considering my age, until it came to navigating the stairs! At this point I fell head over heels to the bottom. Although I could get along in my dad's shoes on the flat, as soon as the terrain changed I became vulnerable and took a tumble. I was simply 'too small for my boots' in reverse to the usual statement. Lacking in maturity and ability to fill out the shoes, I found myself unable to navigate. This so often applies to people who 'want the badge' and 'want it now'.

Too often I am approached by individuals with a business card proclaiming themselves to be 'Prophet John Doe'. Usually such people are not attached a local church, nor are they making a useful contribution. They simply have no place of accountability. Once in Europe I met a young man at the end of the meeting who described himself as a prophet. He proceeded to share with me that, "Last night I cast down the spirit that controls France". I responded by assuring him I would be checking the newspaper to see how his prophetic action had impacted the nation. I have indeed kept a check over the years but am still waiting for signs of an outpouring from God that would surely result from such an action. His claims to be a prophet lack evidential substance.

I believe it was the followers of Watchman Nee who determined to describe prophets as "those who have prophetic ministry" in order to do away with what they considered to be a hierarchical title in the church. There certainly are prophets today, but many who take the title to themselves are frauds and charlatans, abusing the body of Christ and using it as a means for personal gain.

In Revelation 2: 20 Jesus rebukes the church in Thyatira for tolerating the woman Jezebel who called herself a prophet. He refers to the consequences of their being misled as sexual immorality and the eating of food sacrificed to idols. These things happen when churches allow such ministries to operate under their umbrella.

Gaining a certificate

Successful completion of a degree course allows a person to add the abbreviation BA or BSc after their name. They complete the necessary studies and become Bachelors of the Arts or of the Sciences. Those who progress further may gain the title Doctor or Professor. Perhaps it is not surprising that some Christians have copied social patterns and created courses that offer certificates. On completion, attendees are able to wave their decorated pieces of paper under the noses of unsuspecting churches and announce they are now fully qualified prophets.

At the beginning of my army experience I embarked upon a six week training course and learnt the rudiments of military life and discipline. It culminated in a 'passing out parade' that celebrated my now-acquired readiness to begin learning to be a soldier. However, I soon realised it was not skill at learning theory that made a soldier, but only solid experience. Now as I travel the world I hear stories of church leaders who have been badly burned by such 'accredited' ministries. These men and women come and take the floor in church meetings bringing strange prophecies and sometimes great pain to individuals. When challenged they wave their card and tell people they have covering and authority from their head office in the USA. They say of themselves, "We are prophets and no one can question our word".

Accepting responsibility

Being a non-commissioned officer brought a certain level of responsibility that was at times burdensome. Not only did I have to deal with daily routines and matters of discipline but also be accountable for my actions to those of greater rank. On occasions, I struggled to deal with the expectations of those both above and below my status. Being consistent and self-disciplined was essential as I sought to prove worthy of the calling and set a good example to those empowered to lead.

People in positions of leadership are often envied by their subordinates. In the business world, colleagues battle for promotion to win the glamorous prize of authority over others. They smell the ground coffee and pastries that pass by under their noses into the private offices of their managers. If only they could wear a pinstripe suit and lounge in leather chairs all day. If only, if only ...if only.

Unknown to them, the manager sits in the chair wishing she didn't have to work such long hours. She stares resentfully at the window that informs her of yet another glorious day lost to deadlines. Shouted at only an hour ago by the head of marketing for overspending on her budget, she ponders how to give the news to three dedicated members of staff that they have become surplus to requirements.

Being a prophet can also be a lonely experience and if anything is only glamorous for the first ten minutes! There is terrific responsibility in the call and is not to be undertaken without conviction that it is God's voice that has been heard, rather than some inner voice of wishful thinking. It does not happen by waking up one day in the morning and saying, "Ah, I think I will be a Prophet". As mentioned previously a process is involved, containing events and people that contribute to the building of such a ministry.

The calling comes from God himself and is not one that we initiate or seek to grow by reaching a point of spirituality that allows us through the magical door of revelation. Jeremiah was set apart to be a prophet even before birth while Isaiah and Moses received their calling as young men. Interestingly, both Jeremiah and Moses felt unqualified for their respective tasks and reluctant to take them on. The former protested at only being a child immature in speech [27] while the latter complained he lacked eloquence and fluidity in talking.[28]

[27] Jeremiah 1: 4-7
[28] Exodus 4: 10

It appears that neither of them saw any glamour or much appeal in their job descriptions, but only the prospect of embarrassment! Fortunately, qualification comes from the Lord and not from one's own ability or skill.

Not that we are competent in ourselves to claim anything for ourselves, but our competence comes from God. He has made us competent as ministers of a new covenant—not of the letter but of the Spirit; for the letter kills, but the Spirit gives life.
(2 Corinthians 3: 5-7)

A serving nature will also be evident in those called to prophetic ministry. This is well illustrated in the lives of Joshua and Elisha who learnt to serve their mentors long before they had any public recognition. Joshua served from his youth as an aide to Moses[29] as well as having a deep passion himself for seeking after God. Elisha meanwhile was anointed by Elijah to succeed him upon the command of God. Elijah did this by placing his cloak upon the young man which represented the ministry passing on. Elisha responded not by boasting of having received a 'badge of office' but by devoting himself to Elijah which proved invaluable in the long run. [30] He did later operate as a fully-fledged prophet but only after he had tenaciously stuck with his mentor through a number of years of simply serving in the field. Later, in 2 Kings 3: 11 when the king Jehoshaphat required a proven prophet he was informed of Elisha, a man who possessed not only a gift of revelation but also a servant heart: "Elisha son of Shaphat is here. He used to pour water on the hands of Elijah."

Displays of service like these are key to the ability of a prophet to serve the body of Christ and not his own agenda. Those with a prophetic calling are usually best situated alongside those who already have a call and from whom they can receive genuine help. My experience is that a greater release

[29] Numbers 11: 28
[30] 1 Kings 19: 15-21

of gifting comes to those who operate alongside more senior prophetic ministries. For several years I travelled and ministered with prophets who were well-taught theologically as well as being spiritually experienced.

Working with these men helped me to learn the value of the balance between Spirit and Word in the prophetic ministry. They were men who understood Hebrew and Greek and the background of the Bible, but were still able to move mightily by the Holy Spirit in revelation. Exemplified in their lifestyle were integrity and personal love and commitment to the body of Christ. These were imparted to me by working alongside them and being drawn into their discussions as well as by observing them in action. Prophesying with them I found my own revelation and insights were stretched into new areas. There is a principle by which prophetic ministry increases in intensity when there is opportunity to work and walk with those who are themselves strongly prophetic.

Recognition

All believers have a place in the body of Christ which needs discovering and releasing to become fully functional. In his famous discourse in 1 Corinthians 12, Paul recognises that the one body comprises many interdependent parts. Under-performance in any area adversely affects everyone. Although it is wrong to seek acknowledgment for selfish purposes or assuming for ourselves a role we are ill-equipped to handle, it is clearly not beneficial to have no recognition at all.

Instead, speaking the truth in love, we will in all things grow up into him who is the Head, that is, Christ. From him the whole body, joined and held together by every supporting ligament, grows and builds itself up in love, as each part does its work. (Ephesians 4: 15-16)

Human ambition seeks a stage and misleads us into having no time or energy to serve God unless it is according to our own desires and will. Godly ambition desires only to become more effective in that which God has called us to do. Recognition of gifting, by the local church and beyond, releases prophetic people to move among churches with authority. Acceptance enables them to operate with confidence in the role and in their full capability and anointing. Particularly encouraging is the affirmation that comes from those who are themselves prophetic with ministries that are proven and have integrity before God and the Church. God often speaks to Prophets about others who are called to stand in the same ministry at a later date. Elisha's initial recognition came from Elijah, a renowned prophet who was respected widely and who spoke clearly of a 'mantle to be passed on'.

In 2 Kings 2 we read of Elijah being taken up to heaven in a whirlwind. It seems the day was well marked by the companies of prophets that existed in those times. Also being aware of the special occasion, Elisha was not feeling too obedient and accompanied Elijah against his wishes to Bethel, Jericho and then finally to the river Jordan. In both towns the local prophets approached Elisha and enquired whether he knew the Lord was going to take his master away from him today. "Yes, I know" he replied, "but do not speak of it." Fifty men of the company from Jericho followed them to the Jordan and stopped at a distance to see what would happen. As the two were walking and talking, horses and chariots of fire suddenly appeared and took Elijah away. Picking up the cloak that had fallen from the departed prophet, Elisha rolled it up and struck the water with it. As he did so the water divided to his left and right so that he was able to cross over. From the distance, the shout of the approaching prophets reached his ears, "The spirit of Elijah is resting on Elisha." When they arrived they bowed to the ground before him.

It was only Elisha who picked up and swung the mantle of the prophet on the day of Elijah's departure. The company who followed were men who had been raised in prophetic atmosphere and who perhaps had gifting in prophetic ministry. However, they did not have authority to step up to the plate like Elisha. He was called not just to walk in prophetic ministry but to actually be a prophet. The level at which a person operates is not to be confused with his own spirituality or seen as a reward by God for good behaviour. Prophecy is a spiritual gift, not a reward or a fruit to be grasped after and assumed as a spiritual ambition.

11 Taking precaution

Several years ago on a trip to Taiwan we were interviewed by a Christian newspaper. The main point of discussion concerned a prophecy given in one of their high profile cities by a visiting foreigner. The word suggested an imminent invasion from mainland China. Further to this alarming prospect, Christians would be killed and subjected to imprisonment and torture. Aware of the dreadful persecution suffered by Chinese believers, it was not surprising that the church in Taiwan responded dramatically. Many pastors simply left the country and abandoned their homes and their flocks. Individual Christians also deserted their families, homes and businesses to migrate elsewhere.

Our first response was to ask if anyone had received a confirming word. Surely an event of such seriousness would be backed up by more than one source. Their answer however produced nothing of substance. Indeed no one else had anything to say about it at all. Rather bewildered by the apparent naivety of the people who had acted on this prophecy and now sceptical of the source, we suggested they contact the home church of the so-called prophet.
A short time later we found they had done this and received the instruction, "Do not listen to this man. He is rebellious and we don't let him prophesy. Not one single prophecy he made has ever come true!"

The 'prophet' had been invited into a large and influential church without anyone taking the elementary precaution of checking him out with his home church and its leaders. The result of this negligence was great fear and much confusion among the church where he had ministered and also the wider body within the influence of the people. Furthermore, the reputation of the church nationally and of prophetic ministry had been damaged.

In 1997, Hong Kong underwent a transfer of sovereignty from the United Kingdom to the People's Republic of China. Prior to the event a woman with a famous prophetic ministry spoke about a 'blood-bath' on the night of the handover, including the deaths and arrests of many Christians. On the 30th June, I was actually there in Wan Chai on the northern shore of the island. Apart from Prince Charles reading out a farewell speech from his mother and a deluge of monsoon rain, nothing of any note happened. When the prophecy was later questioned, the reply came back: "Ah yes, this was forestalled because of the prayer warriors." The odd assertion here is that God gave the word specifically so that people would pray fervently enough for him to change his mind!

On another occasion, I visited a church where confidence concerning the prophetic was very low. In response to my curiosity the leader explained that a lady in the church was barren and unable to bear children. A visiting prophet had prayed with her regarding this problem and prophesied publicly to her that she would bear a child in twelve months. When the allotted time passed without any sign of conception, they contacted the prophet. He simply replied, "Ah. The baby was born in the heavenlies." Both the lady and the congregation had stored up so much hope that she would give birth. It was therefore no surprise to discover the strength of their struggle to receive anyone who might cause them further harm.

And He was saying to them, "Take care what you listen to." (Mark 4: 24 NAS)

Great damage has been done by people who foolishly prophesied things and then tried to spiritualize their way out of the failure to bring a true word from God. They speak publicly and without reservation on matters of much significance, yet are not subject to correction. This is particularly so for those who operate well-resourced and popular ministries. If the prediction fails to occur, they wriggle out of their hole by claiming a 'higher level' of revelation that accounts for the mishap. These excuses do not bring vindication or enhance reputation but rather bring discredit to both them and all those involved in prophetic ministry. Indeed the entire body of Christ is affected as local churches and church streams need specific and real direction from prophets to enable them to do the works they are called to do.

Protecting the flock

Leaders of local churches have a responsibility to protect those under their care from any ministry that is not authentic. This is especially true of prophetic ministry which, if not in order, can disrupt the lives of individuals and the church itself. It is imperative to evaluate words arising from prophetic ministry. The Scripture tells us to 'take care what we hear'. This is not just what passes through our ears, but what we actually give heed to and act upon.

At the same time, bad experiences can cause leaders to become over-protective and reject prophetic ministries without giving full consideration. There may be practical reasons that delay or negate the outcome of personal prophecy. If a person does not do what God asks then he cannot expect the prophetic word to come to pass. Only Scripture is infallible and will come to pass regardless of anything we do or say.

Encouraging 'return' visits brings greater commitment and accountability to both givers and receivers of prophecies. The Bible tells us that Samuel had a regular circuit of travel in Israel. He did not only operate in Shiloh where his headquarters were, but his ministry covered the whole nation. These extended travels gave him the reputation of being a prophet among the people.

From year to year he went on a circuit from Bethel to Gulag to
Mishap, judging Israel in all those places. But he always went
back to Ramah, where his home was, and there he also judged
Israel. And he built an altar there to the LORD. (1 Sam 7: 16-17)

In my own experience I have attempted to travel regularly
through a group of churches seeking to bring understanding
and application of the prophetic words I have brought.
There have been wonderful results, such as buildings, babies
and ministries becoming reality. It has proved truly exciting
for me as a prophet as well as for those that have received
the words personally or corporately. On the other hand, a
prophet cannot return regularly to places where his ministry
is discredited by those that he has ministered to. It is therefore
good for prophetic ministries to commit themselves to making
a circuit in order to see the long term results of their ministry.

Making mistakes

Occasionally, even the most sincere and gifted prophets get
it wrong. When this happens they are not to be regarded as
those from the Old Testament paradigm whose character
was judged according to every word they brought. Like
any member of the body of Christ prophetic people need
correcting and encouraging when guilty of error. They must
allow their words to be evaluated and take responsibility for
them if they do not come to pass.

Do not put out the Spirit's fire; do not treat prophecies with
contempt. Test everything. Hold on to the good.
(1 Thessalonians 5: 19-21)

Mistakes cause less damage when quickly owned up to.
Prophets need to keep humble and allow themselves to
be humbled under the hand of God to avoid giving the
appearance of spiritual superiority. They should not seek
to divert attention, by making spiritual excuses about their
failure to hear well. To wrongly tell a barren woman that she

would bear a child, only to say later "The Lord shows me the baby was born in the heavenlies" is nothing more than spiritual fraud. It needs exposing as such by leaders and other responsible believers.

Admitting fault can help someone who was trusting what was said, to forgive and be healed of any hurt caused. The bearer of the word should seek God for opportunity to counsel with those who have suffered offence. It is essential not to avoid answering the complaint, shrug off the problem or accuse the person concerned as though it were they in the hot seat. Such actions are due to fear of embarrassment or pride in ministry and treat those injured with contempt. If wrong has indeed been done, prophets need to acknowledge their fault, ask for forgiveness and seek to learn from the experience.

Over more than 40 years of public prophetic ministry, I do not have a perfect record and am the first to acknowledge this. I actually don't know of anyone that has. Like so many others I am simply endeavouring to 'press on toward the mark of the high calling of God in Christ Jesus'.[31] Those with a prophetic call need to be striving to have a reputation that nothing falls to the ground and becomes lost. Time spent in prayer before moving in ministry can be a key to hearing correctly and not merely presenting 'fluff' without substance to those who come seeking a clear word from God.

I am however most happy to say that a very thick file is stored in my office containing many testimonies verifying prophetic words that I have bought to churches and individuals through the years. In fact the writing of this book has come out of a desire to encourage prophetic people to move into the realm of excellence in their gift.

"So it is with you. Since you are eager to have spiritual gifts, try to excel in gifts that build up the church." (1 Corinthians 14: 12)

[31] 1 Corinthians 14: 26-33

Testing a word

Whether delivered publicly or privately to individuals, prophetic words can be tested in a number of ways. First and foremost is the written word of God:

When men tell you to consult mediums and spiritists, who whisper and mutter, should not a people inquire of their God? Why consult the dead on behalf of the living? To the law and to the testimony! If they do not speak according to this word, they have no light of dawn. (Isaiah 8: 19-20)

No revelations from God will contradict or override the Scriptures. During the early 1990s in Canada and the United States, a group of prominent prophetic ministries were touting the idea that 'since we have present word from God, we can ignore the written word if there is any conflict'. Sadly, this was taken up by many sincere Christians and produced disaster in their own lives and those of their churches. There is a responsibility of each Christian to be involved in the process of comparing what is spoken with what is written. It is not enough simply to rely on the leaders or on some prominent figure to look carefully into the prophetic direction given.

Now the Bereans were of more noble character than the Thessalonians, for they received the message with great eagerness and examined the Scriptures every day to see if what Paul said was true. (Acts 17: 11)

Secondly, prophecy is to be weighed by the Spirit of the Lord. When something comes from God there is an affirming 'Yes' in our spirits. Although the inner voice is subject to other influences – and therefore it is wise to be wary – the words of the Lord to his disciples in John 16: 13 should give us much cause for comfort. They were clearly told that the Holy Spirit would guide and help them discern truth. There are times when a word is given that causes a person to shudder inside. Most often this is because it does not witness with the Spirit of God within them. This sense needs to be cultivated and encouraged for it is part of our armour and spiritual radar keeping us ahead of the enemy, the devil and his hordes, who never rest in their efforts to deceive and mislead.

Therefore I tell you that no one who is speaking by the Spirit of God says, 'Jesus is cursed,' and no one can say, 'Jesus is Lord,' except by the Holy Spirit. (1 Corinthians 12: 3)

The Bible tells us that there are three qualities that identify the Holy Spirit as the source of a word.

The Holy Spirit will not curse or speak against Jesus or his authority. Those who claim to prophesy and reject the claims of Jesus to be the only Saviour of the World are actually speaking against Him

Words from the Holy Spirit bring freedom (see 2 Corinthians 3: 17). Even when there is an identification of sin or wrongdoing that needs to be dealt with, He will guide that person into the place of freedom.

The Holy Spirit gives life. As Paul says in 2 Corinthians 3: 6, *"For the letter kills, but the Spirit gives life."*

A third consideration is the person speaking. Sometimes prophecy is nothing more than the outpouring of bitter, rejected people who cannot find a place of ministry in the local church. For many years people who were negative and spiteful were assumed to be prophets. Beware of the parking lot variety who appears on the radar just before or after the corporate church gathering. Casting a quick glance in all directions to check the coast is clear, he ambles up alongside the chosen victim and says quietly, "I have a special word for you. I cannot give it to you in there as 'they' don't recognize my call and reject my words".

Such a person is always looking for a way to rebuke or beat on the church as a proof of his prophetic calling. He is seeking to escape the necessity of having words evaluated and wants to ensnare others in his own rebellion, which can never be a good thing. Earlier, I related the story of the man who said, "I am an Old Testament prophet. I like to cut them off at the knees and leave them bleeding", referring to the church. It was obvious from the man's demeanour that any prophecy leaving his lips would be tainted by his own angry spirit.

Anyone who wants to be a channel for the word of God to others must have a relationship with God and be filled with the Holy Spirit. Operating out of love is required and faithfulness in speaking only what God has given them.

Finally, prophecy needs to be evaluated by those who have prophetic insight. 1 Corinthians 14: 29 talks of two or three prophets speaking and the others weighing what is spoken. This verse brings out the necessity of having experienced prophetic ministries in local churches. The general lack of spiritual discipline and training in this area has resulted in such people being an exception rather than a rule. However, I have had the privilege to minister in some fellowships where these ministries do flourish. A pastor, who does not feel he is strong prophetically, will seek to protect the church by assigning people gifted in this area to evaluate words brought to others. Sometimes entire teams are raised up which both fulfil this role for the leadership and mentor others with rising prophetic ministries.

When two, three or more are hearing the same thing from God then much greater validity is given to what is being said and gives assurance that it is not just a 'loose cannon' firing off a word. Such affirmation places a greater responsibility on individuals, groups and entire churches to act on what has been said.

12 And it came to pass

Once, while travelling in the Orient, my wife and I were passing through a marketplace when some jewellery in a shop window caught her attention. We ventured inside and eventually she became attracted to a pearl necklace. Being aware of the tendency of vendors to overcharge tourists, she readied herself for a spot of haggling and enquired of the price. Perhaps expecting some negotiation, the manageress immediately announced that the pearls were genuine. My wife asked if she might hold the necklace and quietly applied a test that someone else had shown her. A minute or so of silence passed by before she finally looked up and stated quite firmly that the pearls were not genuine. Of course, this did not go down well with the Chinese vendor and we left rather abruptly to the sound of great indignation.

Prophetic words can give the appearance of authenticity, especially when delivered from a charismatic and well-versed personality, magnified by marketing machinery. Sometimes prophecies just seem right because they fit the context of what is happening anyway. Someone may say, "I see the imminent fall of Europe and a new thirst for spirituality!" but any reasonable economist would agree that Europe is in danger of financial collapse. It would be very easy for a socialist to add that such ruin will lead to secular people looking elsewhere for their comfort.

There are also the so-called prophets who speak words of gloom and doom with no way of escape. Their unceasing ominous prophesies never seem to happen and produce nothing but depression in peoples minds. When challenged on non-fulfilment they respond by simply shrugging their shoulders and producing another like the last. With all prophetic words, there are principles that can be applied to help evaluate their importance and veracity.

As the rain and the snow come down from heaven, and do not return to it without watering the earth and making it bud and flourish, so that it yields seed for the sower and bread for the eater, so is my word that goes out from my mouth: It will not return to me empty, but will accomplish what I desire and achieve the purpose for which I sent it. (Isaiah 55: 10-11)

This seems to be an unusual scripture to begin with when we are talking about judging prophetic words, but a foundation needs to be laid by first considering the word of God. It is never spoken without purpose and according to this scripture will not return to him empty. Rather it will accomplish what it was sent to do. John in his writings reminds us of the creativity of a true word from the Lord. In John 1: 1-3 we find Jesus revealed as the Word of God through whom all things were made and through whom the plan of salvation was outworked. God speaks and things happen in creative ways that bring them to pass.

Every word divinely uttered carries power released from heaven to accomplish what is purposed. As such, correctly discerning the authenticity of a word from God will allow us to plan and strategize with confidence. The word 'achieve' in the Isaiah passage means 'to push forward'. Hence, when a word is released from the mouth of God there is a weight that is released from heaven that pushes it forward to accomplish his plan and purpose.

Acts 16: 6-9 gives special insight into Paul being specifically directed by God on his missionary journeys. He and his companions were forbidden by the Holy Spirit to enter Asia and then Bithynia. Instead he received a prophetic dream of a man begging him to go into Macedonia. Struck by the urgency of this appeal for help, Paul responded immediately and made ready to travel with his team and entered there at just the right time. The vision had practical application and resulted in a significant church being planted.

Proven by outcome

The validity of all prophetic ministry and direction is tied up in whether or not the prophetic utterance ultimately brings any realistic outcome. Most worryingly, the nature of this ministry is often caught up in mysticism that sees only 'shadows and types' and has no solid fulfilment individually or corporately. Paul does say in 1 Corinthians 13: 9 that "we know in part and we prophesy in part" and thus do not have total understanding. Only when the ultimate purpose and placement of God in eternity is realised will we see clearly. However, this is no excuse for the low level of revelation demonstrated by many who call themselves prophets. Churches today should be seeing at least some predictions coming to pass. If we actually do have partial knowledge, some of it should be right!

Isaiah prophesied many things that are still being played out, but he also prophesied the healing of Hezekiah and it happened straight away. [32] Agabus was a remarkable New Testament prophet who brought words that were acknowledged to be true since they occurred in the very place and manner foretold. In Acts 11: 28, he predicted a severe famine spreading throughout the Roman Empire. When the event happened during the reign of Claudius, the Antioch church was already prepared for it and therefore able to assist their fellow believers in Judea. What a wonderful testimony! 'This happened,' should constantly be the faith-building contribution of prophets to local churches. Some ministries should even grow and mature to the point that entire communities and nations look to the church and heed her warnings with confidence. In short, prophets need to cross the 'credibility gap' in order to earn the right to 'speak to nations'.

[32] 2 Kings 20: 1-11

The ministry of Samuel had an astounding track record. We are told "The LORD was with Samuel as he grew up, and he let none of his words fall to the ground."[33] These fulfilments were affirmation to Israel that Samuel was indeed a prophet who could be trusted. Elisha was also one known for the accuracy of his words. 2 Kings 6: 9-12 reveals that the king of Israel depended upon him time and time again to gain protection during warfare. The prophet's reputation extended to hostile nations. So enraged was the king of Aram by the regularity with which the Israelites seemed to know his plans, he accused his officers of having a spy within their ranks. One of them responded that they were not guilty but rather the enemy had Elisha the prophet who "tells the king of Israel the very words you speak in your bedroom."

The king of Israel checked and constantly found the intelligence he received to be of high value. At the same time this dimension of spiritual warfare and insight was a great frustration to the enemy with whom he was locked in conflict. The power of true prophetic words to bring direction in warfare against the enemy is multiplied when a reputation for accuracy has been established. Prophets who can be relied on therefore have a very important part to play in advancing the Kingdom and supporting church leaders in their constant battle with the enemy.

Proof in the pudding

Someone may exclaim "That looks so delightful; it simply has to be maniacally dived into and devoured. So what if I'm full?" But I know the propensity of some attractive desserts to fail to satisfy my most demanding of taste-buds. As the saying goes, the proof of the pudding is in the eating! The church in Antioch could validate the words of Agabus. Israel and her enemies could verify the truth of Elisha's revelation. The whole nation acknowledged the truth and of the

[33] 1 Samuel 3: 19-20

pronouncements of Samuel. Key to the success of these prophets is that they were all subject to evaluation. Their spirituality was not used to mask their success or failure to produce a true word. None of them needed to make claims for themselves, for the evidence pointed clearly to them being men who consistently heard from God.

Not that we are competent in ourselves to claim anything for ourselves, but our competence comes from God. He has made us competent as ministers of a new covenant – not of the letter but of the Spirit; for the letter kills, but the Spirit gives life.
(2 Corinthians 3: 5-6)

We live in a time when there are many who aspire to the title prophet. They have a hunger for recognition, not just as one who prophesies but as one who holds the role of a governmental prophet. Every week I read messages and declarations on the Internet from those who are trying to achieve this role, and sadly so many are merely either statements of the obvious, 'these are hard times', or greatly mysterious, 'There is a season within a season that only the elect can see!'

Prophets need to be careful about claiming offices when they clearly lack in credibility. Sadly, believing their own publicity and the applause of others can lead them to greatly misunderstanding their own significance, calling and gift. No amount of promotional activity can replace the real and obvious fulfilment of important prophetic words. Sad to say, there is a dearth of such words in the day in which we live.

More of a focus on accuracy might better be encouraged if there was actually less prophecy in the church. This would allow what remained to be seen as true and authentic revelation. Yet sadly, it is not unheard of for a prophet to be 'bought' by an unscrupulous leader and instructed to say 'something motivational'. I wish I could say that this does not happen! However, I have been almost begged by some leaders

when visiting their churches: 'Say something about a new
building' or 'Talk about a fresh move of the Spirit in our church'.
This is hard for prophets when they are being desperately
pressurised by people, who otherwise have high integrity, to
do something totally wrong and detestable to God himself.

Conditional prophecy

Agabus' prophecy concerning the famine was an absolute
assurance of a forthcoming disaster. It's purpose lay in
releasing finances to assemble the provision that God
sought from and for his people. The required response was
preparation. Unlike this prediction of a specific event, some
prophetic words are accurate but not inevitable. This is
because they are conditional upon obedience and action by
the person or people who receive them. If they do not do
what they are commanded or make any preparations for what
is foretold then how can be the intended outcome? Israel
received many promises from God that were both true and
accurate. "Theirs are the promises" declares Paul in Romans 9
but they did not receive them because "they pursued it not
by faith but as if it were by works".

Failure to take prophetic direction must be one of the main
reasons for disappointment in the results. My experience is
that churches and individuals who really value and apply the
prophetic word to their situation see some amazingly clear
outcomes. Others, who are cynical and always comparing
prophecies and grading them, frequently see nothing and
then complain vehemently. In Acts 13: 1-4 the prophets spoke
specifically that Paul and Barnabas were to be released to
the ministry God had for them. In many churches today this
would not be acted upon. After all, following the prophetic
direction given by the Holy Spirit would jeopardise the
expansion of the local infant church. The instruction was
dependent on the willingness of the people to sacrifice and
release two of their most important and effective workers. It
didn't allow for dilution such as 'release two available men'

or 'release in the dim and distant future' but was specific and required immediate obedience to become effective.

Over the years I have become familiar with a casual attitude toward prophetic words and to prophets in many local churches. There is a prevailing failure to grasp the importance of pursuing by faith the promises that God has made.

For we also have had the gospel preached to us, just as they did; but the message they heard was of no value to them, because those who heard did not combine it with faith. (Hebrews 4: 2)

Prophetic words can be delayed or even nullified by lack of faith in others. Joshua and Caleb were initially unable to enter the land God promised because of others unbelief. When we walk with those who reject and refuse direction, we hazard ourselves and may spend many frustrated years looking for the fulfilment of the word. These two faithful men had a sure word from God which God would bring to pass, but those who accompanied them did not hold firm to the same word that Joshua and Caleb received.

Sometimes a prophetic word may simply run out of time! What do I mean by this? Well, it's possible to have a word that requires us to act in a given timeframe to meet a situation. In the case of the Antioch church they needed to act as soon as they got the word about the famine in Judea. With communications as they were in those days, the risk of not actually being able to help was significant. They could have ended up making their response too late. In evaluating prophetic words it is important to consider 'prophetic windows'.

Unlike biblical prophecy where God's word does not return to him empty, personal prophecy has its limitations. 1 Corinthians 13: 8 tells us that "where there are prophecies they will cease." Some scholars say that the word 'cease' here means to 'lose power'. Eventually all personal prophecy will be fulfilled or will lose power because we have not mixed the word of God with faith.

In the early 1970s I was sent to a city in Southern Alberta to plant a church. This was the time of the Jesus Movement when thousands of young folk in North America transiently covered the country. Most of their time was spent on the streets trying to reach people who would not be found in churches. Co-incidentally, I had received a prophetic word at the time of being sent out that I also should be on the streets and 'bringing in the harvest'. The harvest proved to be scant but had I ignored that word or accepted defeat then, I would not have been in a position to reap when the conditions changed in the early 2000s. The prophetic window of opportunity for the word to work would have 'lost its 'power' or 'forward movement' and not been fulfilled.

We shouldn't say that a word was not from God because it didn't come true in cases where the person receiving the word didn't, or worse, refused to take necessary action in line with the word. 'Fighting the good fight of faith' always implies action, often within the context of time. A good example of this is found in Numbers 13-14 when God first brought the Israelites to the Promised Land. A window of opportunity existed for them to step out in faith and take hold of the word that God had given them. When this time expired without the requisite action, they had to wait yet another 40 years for the window of opportunity to come.

Held back by fear

Prophecy may also be unfulfilled because of being afraid to step out in faith during the time of opportunity that God gives us. One of the traps with judging prophetic words is that we spend more time evaluating than stepping out into what God wants us to do. We can become so cautious that the prophetic window becomes closed. When God spoke prophetically concerning the sending out of Paul and his companions on their epic missionary journey, they acted upon it. There was a witness of the Spirit as well as those prophets that stood by that this was indeed the will of God.

Paul later on had the prophetic encounter with an angel which caused him to change his plans yet again and enter Macedonia. To some it may have appeared that Paul was losing the plot and perhaps doubted his leadership. If aware of this, Paul could have considered his position and took the safer, more acceptable route. Instead he chose not to fear for his reputation but to heed the prophetic direction.

While it is important to carefully judge prophetic words, it is equally important to apply faith and step out into the destiny of God. The difficulties sometimes encountered in weighing a word should not be a reason to do nothing with what has been said. If someone trusts the person from whom they receive and there is no known conflict why not follow the prophecy that is given? In 1 Timothy 1: 18 Paul charges Timothy in keeping with the prophecies previously made about him, so that by following them he may fight the good fight. The encouragement here is that no prophecy should be held back by fear on our part. Such fear can be a result of our self-perception which conflicts with Gods vision and prophetic direction. Believing our own opinions can cause us to draw back from what God has spoken.

Again, if the trumpet does not sound a clear call, who will get ready for battle? (1 Corinthians 14: 8)

God is looking for the prophetic ministry to be a reliable and clear voice that calls his people to battle and also that warns and directs them in warfare against the enemy. The church needs clear direction and sometimes the 'difficulties' are in reality fear about stepping out of comfort zones and into the unknown. Equally, those who are prophetic need to forsake their seeking for adulation and recognition and depend on the Holy Spirit to make them credible. Sometimes they cannot wait to grow up and 'be a man' but the process cannot be hurried. May it be that people can write of prophets in these days 'it came to pass.'

13 Receiving a word

One Sunday morning at a church in Southern California, the ushers took me out by a side door so that I could leave without being harassed. Alas it was not to be so. Just as the car door closed, people suddenly burst out of the main door and ran to my vehicle shouting at the top of their voices "Give me a word"! They banged on the windows and impeded the passage of the vehicle. It was actually quite frightening.

Although such requests are not often made with such force, I hear them regularly in prophetic meetings. it seems that people in charismatic churches are conditioned to 'need a word' in order to proceed anywhere in their Christian lives. Frequently, we already have a word from God but simply don't like it. I went for 16 years without believing in the baptism and gifts of the Spirit but still it seemed God was able to speak to me clearly when I needed to hear. Many prophetic words are wasted because we do not do anything with them but wait with bated breath for them to happen automatically.

Let me ask a question. Supposing you knew that only one such word would ever come your way. Would you regard it as a foundation upon which to construct life and vision or as mere casual encouragement to be stored away in a box of 'maybe' dreams? Receiving a prophetic word even just once in life is a privilege and carries with it a responsibility on our part to co-operate with God to see it fulfilled. He is always 'watching over his word to perform it'. If we activate the word by our co-operation we will find that it becomes effective. We must allow this treasure from God to work in us, for its effectiveness will be dependent on our receptivity. The reality is that something needs to be done: a prophetic word of direction is always conditional and never 'happens by itself'.

Consider the famous parable of the seeds in Matthew 13. In verses 19-23 Jesus describes the seed as "the message about the Kingdom". This message is not only the word of God as revealed in the Bible but also those words breathed by the Spirit through prophecy. The human heart is the soil where the words are planted and depending on the condition of the heart, the words will grow and produce their expected 'harvest'. It is the ground therefore that determines the growth. There are people with such an unreceptive condition that they instantly lose anything that has been sown to the evil one. As Jeremiah 6: 10 says:

"To whom can I speak and give warning? Who will listen to me? Their ears are closed so that they cannot hear. The word of the LORD is offensive to them; they find no pleasure in it."

Some do not refuse to listen but instead get excited for a short while. Now that they have been prophesied over, they become active and pray regularly about it. Perhaps a few appropriate books are purchased and a suitcase packed but then difficulties arise and ever so quickly they lose heart and give up. Others meanwhile are too worried about life and chasing after wealth. Allowing themselves to be overwhelmed by cares and pleasures they ignore or forget the word that God has given them. Being so used to instant gratification means they expect the prophetic word to be the same in its fulfilment. So they ignore the word that bites into their consciences even though they know it has originated from God. Maybe they do obey for a while but only with a grumbling heart and a grouchy face. Asking a teenager to clear up the kitchen and take out the garbage is no different: Note the heavy dragging of the feet as they go! Often there is obedience but no joy which eventually leads to failure.

Crops can yield spectacular harvests when grown in good soil. I knew a young man who had a prophetic word that his whole family would be saved by the Lord. Some would simply have waited for something to happen supernaturally but not him! Every Sunday night he phoned his parents and shared what the preacher had said in his message. In fact he spoke and related to his family as though they were already in the process of being born again. Always the conversation included an opportunity for them to find a doorway into the Kingdom. Within two years his whole family gave their lives to the Lord and the prophecy came true. Did he manipulate it? No! He simply saw that he had a part to play in the plan of salvation in co-operation with the Holy Spirit.

Cultivating good soil

As a child much of my time was spent alone through being constantly ill in the winter time. I developed a great hunger for reading and always had my nose in a book. At meal times my mother needed to call me to the table with increasingly authoritative commands as I was more focused on my interest than my need! Sometimes we feel it more important to pursue our own interests than to listen when God is clearly speaking. Maybe we do not like what is being said, but being receptive without offence on our part is a vital necessity when receiving and being ministered to prophetically.

Mary, after being told by an angel that she would fall pregnant, replied "Be it unto me according to your word."[34] She was more excited about God speaking to her than carrying a penalty of death for being considered an unmarried mother. As Paul stood before King Agrippa he justified his actions by pointing out, "I was not disobedient to the vision from heaven."[35] Earlier Ananias had prophesied to him that he would endure much suffering for the sake of the Gospel, but like Mary, he was willing to receive what God had said and not to discount it because of discomfort. Thus the prophetic word challenges and divides our spiritual heart

[34] Luke 1: 38
[35] Acts 26: 19

from our natural heart or desires. If we are governed by the former we will receive willingly whatever God speaks to us.

Those who gladly received his word were baptized; and that day about three thousand souls were added to them. (Acts 2: 42 NKJV)

Receiving the word with gladness leads to radical change. Baptism in the lives of these early believers was more than simply a church event. The act in itself was a declaration and a challenge to those who watched. Those being baptized were identifying publicly with Jesus who, 'for the joy set before him endured the cross, scorning its shame'.[36] A joyful attitude is essential to a prophetic word taking root in us. We should rejoice both at the privilege of having a personal word from God and also at the opportunity of partaking in the joy that abounds in heaven over every act of glad submission. Jesus saw this joy and it was sufficient to carry him to the cross. It is possible that trial and difficulty may occur because of what God asks us to do but we should still receive with positive hearts. God is looking for joy to fuel the act of obedience and also commitment.

In an earlier chapter, I mentioned prophesying to a church concerning a new building. Two characteristics were that it was brown and formerly used for medical purposes. Also a man would withstand them and cause difficulties. Today they have a wonderful building obtained at a significant discount from the asking price and their church is growing incredibly in the location. This would not have happened if they had not devoted themselves to following through their prophetic word. The same is true for individuals; every person needs to dedicate themselves to doing all that God asks when he speaks. So often we expect his commitment but fail to appreciate our own responsibility in fulfilling what has been said.

There was a prophetic word given to a man named Naaman by the prophet Elisha. It required the humiliating action of

[36] Hebrews 12: 2

dipping himself seven times in a dirty river in order to be healed of leprosy.[37] Acquiring the result involved an ongoing process of commitment. Initially disgruntled, this man was blessed by servants who encouraged him to go into the water all seven times and so he obtained the healing that had been prophetically promised. Like him, we have to hold on and endure in spite of any personal misgivings or even devilish attempts to make us give up.

Finally, the word needs to be received with understanding. There is a measure of how fruitful the prophetic word is going to be and the harvest is often affected by our ability to understand what God is saying. This is not to be confused with what I call 'mystery prophecy'. This is prophecy couched in terms that make it hard to make sense of and open to many interpretations. I once heard a man prophesy words that were very doubtful in their authenticity. After a few weeks the prophecy turned out to be totally the reverse of what actually happened. When I challenged him about the obvious discrepancy he replied, "Haven't you ever heard of reverse prophecy? God gives them to me all the time". This man was a false prophet who used the 'mystery' style to cover his lack of ability to hear from God. If God gives us a prophetic word it will be possible to understand and not couched in such obscure terms that no one comprehends the meaning.

Working it out

Some words may be mostly creative and speak to things we do not yet know we have. I have brought ministry to people who said afterwards, "You got it wrong: I don't have that kind of skill or ability." Once during a prophetic meeting I asserted that a couple present were called to be worship leaders. The response of the crowd was not very positive. The guy could play the guitar but could only sing three notes and two of them were flat! His wife had no musical skills at all. However,

[37] 2 Kings 5: 1-19

both believed the word of the Lord. A year later the wife taught herself to play piano by ear and complement her husband. They worked together and became proficient and later joined another church as worship leaders.

In Genesis when God spoke there was something created, so also with the prophetic word. There is a creativity that makes 'things that are not as though they already were'. [38] In a small Alberta town doing outreach meetings I called a man to the front and prophesied that he would be preaching the gospel and that his family would join him. Roars of laughter came from the crowd, but no one explained them to me. Fifteen years later I got a phone call from a man who recalled the incident vividly as he was the man I had called out. He explained that he was rightly known as the 'town drunk' and had determined to go to church on the one night that I held my meeting. The crowd of course was aware of his reputation and so had burst out laughing. He went on to say that this prophetic word had changed his life and now was a Lay Reader in an evangelical Anglican church. Also his two sons were both in full time ministry. No one except God would have seen the potential in this man but the prophetic word revealed and created it.

In both of the above examples, the length of time between prediction and fulfilment depended to some extent on the actions of the individuals involved. While it is always good to be active, the timing of God may lay beyond our ability to influence. Ecclesiastes 3: 1 points out "there is a time for everything and a season for every activity under the heavens." This is true for prophecy as well. When God promised Abram and Sarah that they would have a child destined to be the 'seed' of a people of faith, it was an exciting time for them. However, since they had already reached their old age it seemed impossible. In order to accommodate the situation they arranged for Hagar, a concubine, to bear a child instead. They lost hope in the timing of God and made a massive mistake.

[38] Romans 4: 17

2 Peter 3 tells us that "With the Lord a day is as a thousand years and a thousand years are as a day" and so we may sense an immediacy or urgency in a prophetic word that God does not. We need to be mindful of this and willing to wait patiently for his timing; even if like Sarah's case it takes a miracle.

For the revelation awaits an appointed time; it speaks of the end and will not prove false. Though it linger, wait for it; it will certainly come and will not delay. (Habakkuk 2: 3)

Impatience can be a big problem. The Charismatic world is full of things bought forth before their time because of unwillingness to let the word mature and come to pass. I have seen people set out to construct church buildings, initiate missions and release people in ministry before the timing of the Lord. All have produced disaster and left many doubting the prophetic words they received.

Patience like that of Joseph is required. Sold as a slave and then falsely imprisoned, he eventually received much more than he expected or understood – all because he waited patiently in faith. He kept a steady head and a true heart for God and every word that he received came true, and more. When I first arrived in Canada, more than 40 years ago, a lady with a strong prophetic mantle foretold that I would be speaking to people of all denominations in their own living rooms. At the time I was involved in the charismatic movement and we held meetings every night in the homes of people of many diverse groups. I interpreted this word in the light of my involvement in one city in Western Canada. Thirty years later I was sitting in a TV studio waiting to do my first televised ministry when the Holy Spirit spoke to me and said, "Now you are going to speak to people of different denominations in their living rooms all across Canada." God is greater than our small thinking and has much more for us than we can ever think.

We need to surrender our own understanding to that of God's, rather than risking the danger of trying to force him into our own time-frame. Gaining a correct perspective can be achieved by praying about our prophetic words and asking God how to interpret them and what actions to take.

Trust in the LORD with all your heart and lean not on your own understanding; in all your ways acknowledge him, and he will make your paths straight. (Proverbs 3: 5)

Although Abram and Sarah attempted to force the issue with regard to timing, they nevertheless believed the prophetic promise. God's delays are not his denials and so we must hold on with faith to what is spoken over us. Hebrews 4: 2 comments that the message has no value unless combined with faith while later in 10: 35-36 we are urged not to throw away our confidence but rather to persevere and receive what is promised.

It is good to have confidence in the prophet who brings the word particularly when he is proven and trusted in the church. However, the focus of our faith should be the Lord himself who is the Author. The prophet is simply the mailman and not the writer of our message from God. The faith we need is not just to become entrenched in our minds but also to be expressed in actions that show we believe what God has said to us. Thus, if we are called to be working in a certain nation or amongst an ethnic group, we can demonstrate our faith by setting out to learn the language and assimilate the culture as a preliminary.

A humble spirit

Having faith requires being sure about what has been spoken to us. To enable this God provides safeguards to keep us from error and also to avoid being misled by vagrant prophets. Anyone who receives a prophetic word should evaluate it with the help and counsel of their pastors, overseers or elders. The Bible calls these men 'shepherds of the flock' for good reason and part of their calling is to check what the ears of the sheep are hearing. Often we have a tendency to only remember the high points of what was said and to reject or overlook disciplinary or corrective comments. Allowing those we trust to help us with insight and counsel is a healthy display of spiritual maturity and may be a golden opportunity to receive the correction and insight we so need.

Churches too should humbly seek counsel with apostolic and prophetic ministries in order to understand and apply words of corporate direction and vision. Too much prophecy lands up unapplied and dusting on a shelf: yet another ornament from a prophetic event they hosted. In marked contrast, churches seeking counsel have received dynamic direction, bringing both stability and explosive growth to their congregations.

Prophetic words are also often complimentary in nature and this should come as no surprise when considering the divinely lavish and gracious heart from which they originate. Their destination however is the heart of sinful man who finds it very easy to become what the Bible describes as 'puffed up'. We should remember that God sees the finished product and does not always speak about us as we presently appear. A positive and powerful word places a responsibility on us to 'purify ourselves'. Simply, we must guard our own heart against conceit and pride in relationship to what God has said.

Therefore, get rid of all moral filth and the evil that is so prevalent, and humbly accept the word planted in you, which can save you. Do not merely listen to the word, and so deceive yourselves. Do what it says. (James 1: 21-22)

A young man called out in a meeting received a prophetic word that he would have an apostolic ministry with great impact in the future. He was one of the wildest young men in his local church and to the listening crowd it seemed an incredible statement. How could he attain to such a calling? Simply speaking he couldn't, not if he stood in his own pride and arrogance. However, by becoming humble and submissive this word may yet become his reality.

The prophetic word is personally planted in the good soil of our heart by the Holy Spirit. Humility and willingness to submit to his calling are keys to the effectiveness of the message received. When God speaks positively of us and gives 'high callings' we must respond with meekness and humility, not pride and arrogance. The initiative is ours to humble ourselves if we want God's destiny to have full impact in our lives. Men like Joshua and Elisha did this and saw in due time that God lifted them up to their ordained calling. It is good to remember that all gifts and ministry come from the Holy Spirit and are not a reflection of our goodness but of his grace.

A weapon of war

Finally, a prophetic word is not just about insight and direction but is a weapon to fight with. Paul charged his protégé Timothy to adhere to the prophecies made about him. In doing do he would be able to fight the good fight![39] There is a guaranteed path to success in our lives and ministries and that is to follow the words spoken over us in prophecy. Rather than employing simply good ideas we have directive words that are powerful in spiritual warfare – as well our enemy the devil knows. We can use these words to resist depression and the discouragement he sends. We can pray and say them out loud when caught in desperation without anything else to cling to.

The weapons we fight with are not the weapons of the world. On the contrary, they have divine power to demolish strongholds. We demolish arguments and every pretension that sets itself up against the knowledge of God, and we take captive every thought to make it obedient to Christ. (2 Corinthians 10: 4-5)

I was driving on the M1 Motorway in the UK on my way to Sheffield. Seemingly out of nowhere a large truck appeared

[39] 1 Timothy 1: 18

just behind me on the outside lane. Suddenly it struck the back of my vehicle and I spun out of control around the front of the truck. The collision crushed the rear and left me sitting inside facing the oncoming traffic at 70mph in the fast lane! As the first vehicle came toward me I remembered a prophetic word that said I would be prophesying over people when I was in my 80s. So I yelled at the top of my voice, "I will still be prophesying when I am 85". Somehow my vehicle ended up in the centre reservation and I along with a companion stepped out totally unharmed! Prophecy is more than a word: it's a weapon.

Prophetic words are very valuable and should not be taken for granted. Many, many believers may go through life solidly on faith, never having received a personal directive word from God. How blessed are we who have received one or more! We need to appreciate and value his promises and to walk in faith in them, knowing they are the key to our victory.

Yet he did not waver through unbelief regarding the promise of God, but was strengthened in his faith and gave glory to God, being fully persuaded that God had power to do what he had promised. (Romans 4: 20-21)

14 It can happen anywhere!

Visiting London is both an enlightening and wearying experience. At various stages of the day the combinations of commuting, sight-seeing and walking extract a heavy price from limbs, particularly if they are walking in their latter stages of life. Frequent rest periods are compulsory and best enjoyed away from the crowds of tourists and pin-striped workers marching mercilessly at high speed. Even the high-heeled business women are dangerous and will not change their paths should one be unlucky enough to obstruct them.

So it was I found myself sitting in St Paul's Cathedral and taking a breather. The surroundings were immense and seemed strange in their spacious grandeur set amidst the hustle and bustle outside. A glance up towards the lofty ceiling of the dome revealed the words of the Psalmist exhorting those below to 'Praise God in his Sanctuary'. Almost involuntarily I began to quietly sing "Be exalted oh God above the heavens" (a popular worship song at the time). Within seconds of heeding the psalm, a hand gently rested upon my shoulder and the voice of a somewhat gloomy verger interrupted: "Please be quiet sir. This is a church you know!"

In this historic and famous building, the setting for many great occasions considered to be sacred, a depressive atmosphere pervaded – more in keeping with a library and feeling somewhat secular. Many grand old cathedrals of worship are the same: their bells freely ring out a call to worship but inside the walls demand religious conformity. "We have a way of dong things in here" they whisper. "Use the words of our official hymn book when praising God and do it at the right time. The next service of worship is at 7am."

It is also easy to develop a pattern of thinking that the place of prophecy belongs uniquely within church meetings and requires a specially anointed atmosphere. Although this is not true, it is however the context within which prophetic gifts can be validated and nurtured before being 'let loose' on an unsuspecting world.

More than Sunday morning

The church owes a debt to Saint Patrick who demonstrated in his thinking and writing that there should be no difference in behaviour between being in the sacred and the secular world. We don't move out of one and into the other like they are separate universes. Understanding this concept will affect our attitude to what we call 'secular' and what we view as 'spiritual' locations. Often we mistakenly associate the word 'church' with a building or formal gathering of believers, rather than people who together comprise the church.

Moses was faithful as a servant in all God's house, testifying to what would be said in the future. But Christ is faithful as a son over God's house. And we are his house, if we hold on to our courage and the hope of which we boast. (Hebrews 3: 5-7)

The majority of gatherings we read about in the book of Acts did not take place in buildings set aside and dedicated to the work of God. Most of Jesus' teachings took place in the open air or in intimate scenes such as around the table at the home of Mary, Martha and Lazarus in Bethany. Moreover, many of Jesus' miracles and those of the early church occurred at 'street level' as demonstrations of divine power right before the eyes of an incredulous public. In Acts 3: 4-10 Peter and John are on their way to the temple when a beggar calls out to them for help. Normally people just passed by looking the other way, pretty much like they do in modern cities. But not today. These two men, perhaps highly focused on their destination, took time to pause and look him straight in the eye. I wonder how many of us would have stopped and allowed such an interruption to our schedules? Sadly we are often too self-concerned to allow for sudden compassion and so deny God the opportunity to bring a timely word of liberation or even a miracle. "I don't have any money" Peter told him, "but what I do have I give you. In the name of Jesus Christ of Nazareth, walk."

It's not just the confidence with which he spoke that is so striking but also the willingness to take a risk. Yet this was no spontaneous act of recklessness that gambled on 'divine backup' and displayed no concern for reputation. Rather it was the response of a man who recognised the prompting of the Holy Spirit and acted accordingly. The past few years had been spent with Jesus and the other disciples who were in effect his local church. With them he witnessed firsthand how Jesus spent time praying with his Father, keeping an open channel of communication that meant God's voice could be clearly heard at all times and in all situations. "I only do what I see my Father doing"[40] he heard Jesus tell the Jewish leaders. Peter saw Jesus speak with authority and as one who expected his words to occur. When the 'Twelve' were sent out in Mark 6, Peter was among those endowed with authority to drive out demons and perform healings. What he learnt to do within his 'church' became a way of normal life. Acts 10 records him visiting the house of Cornelius the Centurion after a prophetic vision from God. Once again the setting was neither a church meeting nor under a 'special anointing', yet the Spirit of God broke out powerfully as he spoke.

Once on my way to an engagement in the US I had to stop overnight in a city in Montana. Alone for the evening, I found a restaurant advertising "all you can eat fish and chips" and proceeded to a table with the intention of fully exploring the depths of the offer. While the task was in full swing, after a plate or two had disappeared, the Holy Spirit began to deflect my attention towards two men sitting in the far corner. They were talking very earnestly and quietly but as I sat there more and more revelation filled my mind. Finally, I knew that

[40] John 5: 19

I needed to go and speak with them but initially resisted using the excuse of being very 'dressed down'. Even the camel-haired clothing of John the Baptist had nothing on my leather jacket, flat cap and old jeans. After deferring as long as possible – and another plate – I crossed the room and stood by their table. "Excuse me gentlemen," I interrupted quite nervously. "I am a prophet and feel that God has given me a message for you." After a few moments of surprised silence, one of them replied "Sit down here please. We are believers and willing to hear what you have to say". For the next ten minutes I shared the insights that God had given me concerning them and the situation they were discussing. "Are you sure you weren't sitting at our table said the older man? These things are the very things that have been perplexing us and about which we have been talking about for so long!" Just as in the house of Cornelius, no music or worship team were on hand to produce the 'atmosphere' for prophetic ministry.

Onto the streets

Today many churches are doing 'Treasure Hunts' and similar things that take people to the streets to encounter people on a spiritual journey that has so far not included entering a 'sacred' building as part of the quest. On one occasion, a church leader who oversaw some ten million 'underground' believers in China asked me this question: "Brother Keith would you please come to my country and teach our people about spiritual gifts?" Somewhat taken aback I replied, "Surely you don't need my help in that area?" To this she answered, "We send our prophetic people out on the street with an evangelist. When the prophetic one senses an open heart he points the evangelist to them and they get saved! However, we don't understand it from the Bible!" Finally I responded, "We understand it from the Bible and don't do it! You are better off than us. It is us who need your help!"

Prophets with whom I worked in the 1980s and1990s would mostly have been horrified at the thought of sharing their gift in a 'worldly' situation without the accompaniment of a worship band and an attentive, properly-dressed crowd. For the most part they had little concept of their gift in the marketplace, regarding what they had as holy and in need of protection. I am not going too far in saying that for many then – and some today – the concept would have been considered as 'casting your pearls before swine'.

The church today faces a great challenge in accepting that the world does not in general come to its door looking for the answers to life. They certainly are not looking for a demonstration of the supernatural. Instead they go for a palm-reading or psychic interview to have a mysterious encounter in the paranormal field. They hope to illuminate their past and be told their future – even change it by following a prescribed course of action. The thought of visiting a local church on their supernatural quest does not occur to them. Yet the fact of their hunger is undeniable, for God has created a curiosity in the hearts of mankind so that all would seek him.

He has made everything beautiful in its time. He has also set eternity in the hearts of men; yet they cannot fathom what God has done from beginning to end. (Ecclesiastes 3: 11)

Often people are not actively searching for greater meaning, in fact they rarely stop to give it much thought. However, when something outside of their normal experience occurs, a previously hidden urge to know more and respond is quickly aroused. Consider the Samaritan woman in John 4 who is going about her daily business when one day she meets a stranger at the well. A quick glance tells her that he's a Jew and therefore they will ignore each other. That was the prevailing culture and one which still continues today. Back then the tension was over Mount Gerizim or Jerusalem as the place to worship. Now it's not only religious arguments but also political and commercial ones that drive nations and even communities apart. Even living in certain districts or supporting different football teams can be reason for conflict. The Samaritans and the Jews had settled on non-association: they simply didn't speak to each other. But this stranger crossed the line. More than that, he told her things that naturally speaking he couldn't know.

Are we prepared to go to those we normally wouldn't approach? Whether they belong to a different generation, race or religion, the church and every individual therein are called to reach every tongue, tribe and nation. The stranger swept past the barriers and relayed to this woman the exact number of her failed marriages and current relationship status. This meeting was seemingly by chance but one that would dramatically affect her and hundreds of others. Encounters with Jesus always provided people with a reason to think and perhaps even to change.

Revelation brings salvation

Prophetic words delivered outside of church meetings are much closer to what is known in charismatic circles as 'words of knowledge'. They differ from prophecy given to churches and individuals in the context of the local assembly. These words require a growing maturity and an intensity to receive and deliver what is strategic and directional in nature. It is also worth noting that prophets are not confined to the gift of prophecy but also move powerfully in words of knowledge to gain the attention of those to whom they are speaking.

Prophesying 'on the streets' is becoming more common, as believers are rediscovering what it means to walk in the Spirit in their daily lives. It is a response to his promptings to point people towards Christ. Words delivered under the specific direction of the Holy Spirit are for the benefit and conviction of those who do not yet know the Lord.

The unfolding of your words gives light; it gives understanding to the simple. (Psalm 110: 130)

This verse is usually and correctly connected with the power of Scripture in our lives. However, it also goes beyond this and applies to any way in which God speaks to us. The prophetic word brings understanding to people that confirms he is real and knows them personally.

The restaurant, the street, the store, the school, the bus all are good places to respond to the Holy Spirit. My wife Nova and I were in a furniture store when a ridiculously bizarre chair caught our gaze. it looked like two buckets on top of each other with a cut-out to allow you to sit down. I commented on this and we passed by on to something else. On the way back we passed the chair again but this time a man from Africa was sitting on it. Suddenly quickened by the Holy Spirit I turned in his direction and looked him in the eye. "Hail to the King!" I exclaimed with my hand raised in salute. With wide eyes he returned my gaze and asked who told me that? I responded, "Who told me what?" His reply: "That I come from the village where the kings are crowned?" This opened a conversation where I explained to him that I had heard a message from the King of Kings and Lord of Lords.

A young Chinese woman was bought to me for prayer by a friend. She came with some hesitation and displayed an obvious uncertainty. But this changed when the Holy Spirit showed me a picture of her in great distress and hiding in a room. Then the picture changed to her running and running and running. At this point she began to speak rapidly in Mandarin. The interpreter explained to me, "She says if Jesus knows me that well I must give my life to him now." The rest of the story? She was a student in China and had gone with many others to Tiananmen Square and observed the deaths of many of her fellow students in a barrage of gunfire. Terrified she ran to her room and lay hidden for several days, dreading the knock of the Secret Police. After three days she gathered her few possessions and ran away until she reached Hong Kong and from there travelled to America.

Opening the heart

Revelation that results in salvation should be a normal part of church meetings that attract those who are not yet Christians; especially when prophetic people are active.

But if an unbeliever or someone who does not understand comes in while everybody is prophesying, he will be convinced by all that he is a sinner and will be judged by all, and the secrets of his heart will be laid bare. So he will fall down and worship God, exclaiming, "God is really among you!" (1 Corinthians 14: 24)

While ministering in what I call our 'home church' in Taiwan the Lord impressed upon me to go and stand beside a young lady in the congregation. As I laid hands on her and began speaking, I discerned that she was quite oppressed. I began to describe this condition of depression and the tears flowed down her face. The Lord then showed me that she worked closely with individuals every day and this was connected to an ability to use colours. I saw a palette of colours in her hands and that all day she was working with blending and matching them. She was in great distress at this point and one of the co-workers came and took her away for prayer and counsel. As it turned out, she was an intellectual Buddhist who had come to the meeting to observe and see if Christianity had a supernatural element. Her occupation was as a make-up artist that involved choosing the right colour combinations for her customers all day. She was suddenly faced with supernatural revelation which caused her to realize that Christianity was more than an intellectual thesis. That night she gave her life to Christ and laid aside her previous religious affiliations

In Norfolk in the UK, I was speaking in a meeting when a man came in through the door who immediately caught my attention. Finally, I could no longer concentrate on my message because of the urgency of this man's need. Calling him to the front I began to share the revelation of the Holy Spirit to him. God showed me he was a man on a quest, a journey of discovery. He had gone down many roads seeking the supernatural without success but was still looking, still seeking. God then showed me some details of his family life which I recounted and he confirmed them all as true. Thus emboldened I ventured, "Has this convinced you of the supernatural in Christianity?" He responded positively and immediately received Christ as his Saviour. It turned out that this man was a Professor of Philosophy at a University. For many years he had explored the various spiritual and religious avenues that his job exposed him to in a vain search for the supernatural reality of God. He had even tried good evangelical churches, where the lack of the manifested presence of the Holy Spirit had led him to believe Christianity was not in fact supernatural.

The power of prophetic ministry in both the marketplace and in the church is indeed a great tool for evangelism. Its value has been underestimated for far too long. While much blessing results from the church publicly proclaiming the Gospel, prophetic revelation enhances the blessing by providing a direct avenue to the heart of man through the Holy Spirit. As the Samaritan woman went on to exclaim to her fellow villagers: "Come, see a man who told me everything I ever did. Could this be the Christ?"

15 Speaking to the bones

It used to be the case that continually speaking to yourself was an obvious sign of mental imbalance. Nowadays I'm not so sure. The young man with air-pilot headphones boogies along the sidewalk, singing not-so-sweet melodies to himself while passing by a new mother. She in turn is pushing a buggy and crooning rhetorical questions into a mass of blankets. I hear ladies in department stores loudly deliberating with their mirror reflections over clothes and men having full-blown arguments with invisible versions of themselves. But if some traits of modern behaviour are odd, what about speaking to bones as Ezekiel was instructed to do?

The hand of the LORD was upon me, and he brought me out by the Spirit of the LORD and set me in the middle of a valley; it was full of bones. He led me back and forth among them, and I saw a great many bones on the floor of the valley, bones that were very dry. He asked me, "Son of man, can these bones live?" I said, "O Sovereign LORD, you alone know." Then he said to me, "Prophesy to these bones and say to them, 'Dry bones, hear the word of the LORD!' (Ezekiel 37: 1-4)

Ezekiel lived at the edge of what was usual and acceptable for a prophet in his day. Blessed with great prophetic insight, we find him caught up in a vision that revealed the destiny of devastated people who felt rejected and without hope. Before him lay heaps of dry bones scattered in a valley where the prospects for any kind of natural growth looked poor. It seemed almost that God wanted to emphasize the dryness by given him plenty of time to wander around and get a real feel for just how long they had lain there. Every last drop of moisture was gone and soon they would be dissolving into dust. Perhaps with that very thought deeply impressing his mind, God asked him "Can these bones live?" Ezekiel was smarter than most and replied "Lord, only you know that."

The story unfolds with the prophet speaking to the bones. Before his eyes the breath of life enters and re-shapes them into a vast army. It doesn't happen all at once but in stages. You can almost imagine his astonishment as the bones start to move together into human shapes. His heart must have missed a beat at the sound of the large rattling but what came next was even more unnerving. Tendons emerged upon their surface, like soft green buds that somehow sprout from gnarled branches. Next came the growing of flesh until the bones were covered and the unmistakable form of man became apparent. Many men now lay before him, but as naked corpses strewn everywhere across the ground. But still there was no life. Even with skin and every vital organ in place, no chest heaved from breathing the air. They were no closer to that than when laying as a mass of dry bones. Ezekiel was commanded to prophesy again. And now they rose, completely restored – a vast army standing before him, alive by the resident Spirit of God.

Whenever discouraged with prophetic ministry, I think of this startling vision and remind myself that God's plan for his people remains the same. The role of New Testament prophets is to keep on 'speaking to the bones' and release the breath of God into the church. If this were no longer needed then there would have been no Agabus nor mention of prophets alongside apostles, evangelists, pastors and teachers in Ephesians 4. The ministry exists so that reviving life will enable us all to stand on our feet like a great army and accomplish the purposes of God. Consider the nature of breath: a constant inhaling and exhaling of air. The purpose of maintaining life remains the same but each breath is new. Similarly, the plan of salvation and a glorious church is unchanging but every day fresh opportunities for growth abound. People need to be told the gospel and brought to maturity in Christ in ways that are unique to them. Prophets have a vital part to play in this and the verses from Ezekiel also remind me that this goal is achieved step by step.

Growth in stages

Once when visiting a church in the American Midwest I stayed in the home of an elder and was asked after supper whether I would like to see his new garage. Feeling rather contented in a comfortable armchair and unable to think of a suitable excuse, I reluctantly agreed and lumbered towards an area at the rear of the house. When we arrived I looked in vain for a garage. Finally, having extracted sufficient amusement from my puzzled expression, he laughed and pointed to some piles of bricks and grinned, "I haven't actually built it yet but I have all the raw material and am working on it one project at a time".

As Ezekiel stood in the valley he beheld what must have looked like chaos after he prophesied. Prophetic words when initially given to a church often do have this effect when they involve major transition. But it was God who prompted him to speak and this was the driving force, as it should be for prophets today. We are not responsible for what might happen when giving a 'bones to body' word, only for delivering it. Just as his words initiated a series of 'projects' that followed each other in logical stages, so ours may too. I find it most exciting to see change occurring in stages after prophesying and have been amazed to see churches gradually emerge from years spent totally steeped in legalism and tradition. One prophetic word can sometimes do more than a thousand sermons to bring change to a congregation.

When churches respond to such words as we have seen them do in Europe and Asia, something definitely happens! It gets noisy, sometimes with controversy, but things start to come into place. A skeleton is really the shape of the body to which other elements are added. After the tendons, Ezekiel saw flesh appear. Skin is what gives shape and beauty to the body and also recognition. Without skin we would look like raw meat and scarcely know one person from another. It can be viewed as representing New Testament church government being released into the church as prophetic ministry identifies those called to various roles of leadership. This gives the local church identification and shape that is, by itself, an attraction to those outside its walls.

The prophetic word can also release relational strategy in the local church especially among the leaders. Many years ago I was invited by a group of people intent on beginning a church to minister and 'speak to the bones'. In the course of the meeting God clearly showed me two couples whom he was calling into long term relationship in the leadership of a new fellowship. Those around them were a little surprised. But twenty years later that foursome still lead a dynamic church where their relational demonstration has released other groups in their church in relational team ministry that stretches well beyond their own nation.

Finally Ezekiel saw the evidence of his own prophecies standing before his eyes. The sight of a great breathing army is the culmination of the prophetic vision that God has given for his church in the last days. This is the army that will do mighty exploits and bring salvation to the nations. Speaking to the bones is very important! It is the source of change and of the re-tooling of the church to reach a new and entirely different generation. This may sound triumphalistic but this is God's ordination:

That at the name of Jesus every knee should bow, in heaven and on earth and under the earth, and every tongue confess that Jesus Christ is Lord, to the glory of God the Father. (Philippians 2: 10-11)

Through God's eyes

Ezekiel's vision arrived during a time of exile in Babylon. Torn from his native land and forced to live in a foreign environment, he was entrusted with bringing God's message to his people. Although the nation of Judah had brought this disaster upon themselves, God had not abandoned them. In the short term everything appeared gloomy but the bigger picture brought hope and was something worth living for. It made the ridicule and ill-treatment bearable. Inspired by the words of Ezekiel they could begin to face up to their sin and return to a God who still loved them. It is still the case today as we look out on a church that appears like 'heaps of dry bones', full of mountainous divisions fuelled by personal ambition, jealousy and false doctrine. Sometimes the idea of light at the end of the tunnel appears preposterous, almost laughable when enveloped in darkness but our focus needs to be fixed on what God sees and not the current situation. No matter how much the tide of evil seems to be gathering momentum in every country and sucking passion and life out of so many believers; no matter how dry some of us may feel, the church is still the instrument by which God intends to carry out his purpose on the earth.

His intent was that now, through the church, the manifold wisdom of God should be made known to the rulers and authorities in the heavenly realms. (Ephesians 3: 10)

As we only "know in part and prophesy in part"[41] a complete comprehension of how God will do what he has promised is not ours to have. However, what we do know is that there is a part to play with our knowledge. Yes we will occasionally shudder with despair and unbelief in our struggles but nevertheless we must live in the expectation of seeing the prophetic plan of God come to full fruition. The people needed to hear of Ezekiel's vision regardless of how much he understood it. The fact that he had to obey a command to speak to the bones would also have brought home to him his role amongst the people. If he did not speak then nothing would happen. The message being conveyed was therefore

[41] 1 Corinthians 13: 9

not just of future restoration but also of the need for his active participation. Responsibility lay upon him to keep hearing from God according to his calling and to keep speaking. Did God need Ezekiel to speak as if he was lacking in any way? Of course not, but as with all ministries and all believers, God chose to act in partnership with the frail man before him.

Prophets and churches alike need to take note of this. We may not understand or even like prophetic ministry, particularly as faith is required in embracing words from God. Faith rarely comes cheaply, for as the writer to the Hebrews says: "faith is being sure of what we hope for and certain of what we do not see."[42] Stepping out into the unknown requires boldness and confidence in our Father who has chosen to use prophecy as a means of communication with his people. To devalue this gift or confine it to the Old Testament is to miss out on the breath of God for today. As Jesus explained to the Sadducees, "God is not a God of the dead but of the living".[43] It makes no sense that he would stop talking to his people and giving them strategic direction. The resurrection of Jesus and the sending of the Holy Spirit brings this gift into the Church for our blessing, alongside the others we so readily acknowledge. Let us therefore embrace it with arms open wide with a hunger to hear, to weigh ...and to act!

Let me finish by asking a few questions. Are you a prophet? If so, then are you on the fringes, wandering around the edge of church and shooting off rounds of prophecies – mostly gloomy – before sweeping off at speed into the cover of the bushes? You should be immersed in a local church, accountable to leaders and hanging around to see your words bear fruit. Are you a pastoral or apostolic leader, perhaps a senior elder? Are you handling prophetic ministry like a hot potato, maybe because of pat misconceptions or some form of abuse you've witnessed or suffered in the past? You can't

[42] Hebrews 11: 1
[43] Mark 12: 27

throw the baby out with the bathwater. The gift is a powerful weapon that God means you to have and to use within your leadership circles and amongst the churches you protect and guide. Finally, you may not be a prophet or a leader but all can prophesy and certainly all can be prophesied over. Are you prepared to step out and be a channel for God to open up someone's heart with a revelatory word – and what about to someone who doesn't even believe in God? Sometimes he gives us something to say to them too! And if a prophetic word does come your way that requires your action, what are you going to do about it? Too many words lay gathering dust on shelves or behind the locked door of fear and low self-worth. If God believes in you, which he does, then why can't that word fit you like a glove? I mean, God using ordinary people – isn't that what it's all about?

Christ himself gave the apostles, the prophets, the evangelists, the pastors and teachers, to equip his people for works of service, so that the body of Christ may be built up until we all reach unity in the faith and in the knowledge of the Son of God and become mature, attaining to the whole measure of the fullness of Christ. (Ephesians 4: 11-13)